Escaping Religion

Vaughn Martin

D1595816

MORE OF
JESUS
Publishing

ISBN: 0-9787875-6-0
ISBN-13: 978-0-9787875-6-1

CONTENTS

VAUGHN MARTIN

PREFACE

I am writing this book out of a deep conviction that the religious systems of the Mennonite church and other denominations are about to be shaken to the point of collapse. At the same time, God is raising up His sons and preparing them for the final harvest.

If you are a Mennonite, this book is for you. I believe that God has a specific call upon the Mennonite church to walk in the footsteps of their ancestors, to take up their cross and follow Jesus. I believe that this calling is far more radical than people understand. It is a calling to be led by the Spirit of God, to preach the gospel with power and boldness in the nations of the earth. It is a calling to walk in the same wholehearted commitment that the early Anabaptists walked in as they gave their lives for what they believed.

If you are not a Mennonite, this book is for you. The things that are taking place in the Mennonite denomination are taking place in many denominations. Many denominations are deeply divided. Ordinary church members continue to believe in the faith of their fathers. They continue to believe in the foundational truths of Christianity and in the authority of the Word of God. However, in the denominational educational institutions, radical change is taking place. College professors in "Christian" colleges frequently work to destroy the faith of their students. "Christian" college professors no longer teach the truths of Christianity. They have become the disciples of the religion of political correctness, and they preach their religion with great zeal.

Quite simply, the educational institutions of many denominations have been hijacked by the enemy. The educated elite of a denomination are trained in these schools, and they begin to transform the denomination into something very different from what it once was. This transformation is taking place in many Christian denominations, including the Methodists, Baptists, and Assemblies of God.

The only significant difference between what is happening in the Mennonite church and other denominations in America is that in the Mennonite church both sides of the divide would generally believe that Christians should not participate in military service. In other denominations, the liberal side of the divide may adhere to pacifism, but the conservative side generally would not.

The examples in this book are largely drawn from the Mennonite denomination, but the message of this book is for a much wider audience. In our times, the religious structures are being shaken, and God is raising up His sons.

INTRODUCTION

On November 6, 2014, 96-year-old Chester Wenger, a former missionary to Ethiopia, wrote an open letter to the Mennonite Church that he had served for most of his life. Chester carried some very impressive credentials. He was a lifelong student and teacher of the Word of God, working for many years as a pastor, Bible teacher, and missionary in different nations. He was instrumental in starting the largest Mennonite church in the world, the Meserete Kristos Church of Ethiopia. Now, in the twilight of his life, he released a heartfelt message to his beloved church. Here are some excerpts from his letter:

An open letter to my beloved church by Chester Wenger

"I am profoundly reluctant to write this letter because I know there are those it will wound deeply. But I have also come to the conviction that I can no longer hide the light the Lord has lit within me, under a bushel. I want to share with you what the Lord has been telling me and my dear life companion.

"My life has been filled with much joy seeing God at work in numerous settings. God's grace has been shown daily on my behalf. But as the Apostle Paul has said so well, "whatever were gains to me I now consider loss for the sake of Christ. What is more, I consider everything a loss because of the surpassing worth of knowing Christ Jesus my Lord, for whose sake I have lost all things.

"The world we live in is no longer the idyllic Eden. It is a broken, complex, messy, violent and yet wonderful world. God's mercy-filled grace infuses our broken world with a goodness that keeps surprising us with joy—and healing. God's grace also calls us to faithfully love God and neighbor above all else.

"The church we belong to has the power to bind and loose. Today's church, much like the early Christians, has the Spirit-given power to rethink whether "circumcision" will continue to define who is in and who is out.

"Because of the brokenness of all sexualities that abuse, lust, access pornography, have sex with unmarried partners of the same or the other gender—because of this brokenness, the church must rise up to reclaim a Godly and wholesome sexuality:-a Godly sexuality that is wholesome because it is covenanted, accountable to and blessed within the church (not left to fend for itself outside the church);

-a Godly sexuality that is wholesome because it calls everyone to recommit our bodies (whether heterosexual or homosexual) to be temples of the Holy Spirit, seeking first the kingdom of God and covenanting to follow Jesus every day.

"When my wife and I read the Bible with today's fractured, anxious church in mind, we ask, what is Jesus calling us to do with those sons and daughters who are among the most despised people in the world—in all races and communities?

"What would Jesus do with our sons and daughters who are bullied, homeless, sexually abused, and driven to suicide at far higher rates than our heterosexual children?

"My wife and I are devoted to our Lord, with a firm commitment to the authority of the Scriptures. We strive to be faithfully obedient to Jesus.

"We invite the church to courageously stake out new territory, much as the early church did. We invite the church to embrace the missional opportunity to extend the church's blessing of marriage to our homosexual children who desire to live in accountable, covenanted ways.

"We know that while many of us hear different things from the Scriptures, God's deepest desire, as made known in Jesus Christ, is "to seek and to save that which was lost." We believe this is an opportune moment for the church to boldly proclaim a pastoral, grace-filled readiness to include both homosexuals and heterosexuals within the blessing of a marriage covenant designed to be wholesome and God-honoring.

"This is the light that has been burning more and more brightly under my bushel, and I am now prepared finally, as a 96-year old, still zealous missionary, to let it shine. So ...

"When the laws of Pennsylvania changed in July, our gay son and his committed partner of twenty-seven years went immediately to apply for a marriage license. Subsequently they asked me if I would marry them. I happily agreed. We held a private ceremony with only six persons present. Our son and his partner are members of an Episcopal Church, but they chose my wife and me to share with them in this holy covenant of marriage." [1]

OPEN UP THE CHURCH BY REDEFINING GODLY SEXUALITY

In this letter, Wenger declares that the church carries an authority to determine who is "in" the church, and who is "out". The early church opened the doors to uncircumcised Gentiles as they were directed by the Holy Spirit, and the modern church needs to open its doors to homosexuals under the direction of the same Holy Spirit.

In this letter, Wenger defines godly sexuality as "covenanted, accountable to, and blessed within the church (not left to fend for itself outside the church)." In other words, when two homosexuals enter into a marriage covenant with one another that is blessed by the church and accountable to the church, they are participating in godly, wholesome sexuality. Their bodies become the temple of the Holy Spirit as they commit themselves to one another and to the Lord.

In other words, homosexuals should not be forced to live out their relationships outside the blessing of and accountability to the church. They should bring their relationships inside the church, into the holy

---

[1] https://themennonite.org/opinion/open-letter-beloved-church/

5

covenant of marriage. These marriages should be recognized by the church as being holy covenants blessed by the church.

In this letter, Wenger declares that the Lord has lit a light within him and given him biblical and spiritual revelation concerning the issue of gay marriage. He writes, "This is the light that has been burning more and more brightly under my bushel, and I am now prepared finally, as a 96-year old, still zealous missionary, to let it shine." In his words his view of these issues is not merely an opinion: it is the light of Christ that he is sharing with his beloved church.

DRASTIC CHANGE IN THE MENNONITE CHURCH

There are few Mennonite leaders who have served the church to the degree that Chester Wenger has. There are few who have seen the results in their lives that Chester has in his. When a Mennonite leader of Wenger's caliber puts all his weight behind the cause of gay marriage, a radical change has taken place.

Chester Wenger is not alone. The Mennonite denomination has changed with him. Until recent years, the Mennonite denomination has been known around the world as a very traditional, Bible- believing denomination. Mennonites have been known as a group that rejected the winds of modernity. Some groups of Mennonites are so traditional that they reject even the use of modern appliances. Many Mennonite groups wore distinctive forms of dress, such as head coverings for the women, and black hats for the men.

Mennonites were willing to be different. Because they believed that the Bible forbids their participation in military service, they refused to participate in military service. Because they believed that the Bible instructs them to dress differently than the surrounding society, they dressed differently. If this made them seem odd and unusual to others, that was just the price that Mennonites were willing to pay to be faithful to Word of God. It was more important for them to be faithful to their understanding of the Scripture than to be acceptable to the surrounding society.

Although these extremely traditional groups of Mennonites still exist today, there has been an overwhelming change in the more mainstream Mennonite groups. The largest Mennonite denomination is Mennonite Church USA (MCUSA). Most of the Mennonites and the Mennonite leaders that make up this group have changed dramatically during the past forty years.

In 2015, Elizabethtown College sociology professor Conrad Kanagy released dramatic discoveries of his findings on the Mennonite Church's view of homosexuality. In 2006, 14 percent of credentialed Mennonite Church USA leaders declared that they would accept a practicing homosexual as an ordained leader in their congregation. According to Kanagy's 2015 research, 46 percent of credentialed leaders declared that they would support the ordination of a practicing homosexual in their congregation.[2]

Fifty-three percent of credentialed leaders believed that a practicing homosexual should be allowed to become a member of their congregation. Some leaders thought that full membership should be allowed without any conditions placed upon a practicing homosexual, while others thought that a practicing homosexual should be in a committed, monogamous relationship before he/she was granted membership.

This represents an enormous alteration of the Mennonite denomination. Generally speaking, when people change their views on homosexuality and gay marriage, they change their views on many other things as well. The person who believes that gay marriage is a holy institution has probably changed his views on the authority of Scripture. There are a number of Scriptures that condemn homosexual sin in extremely strong terms, an element that we will discuss later. The person who believes that gay marriage is holy needs to find a way to get around these Scriptures. He either finds a way to interpret these Scriptures in a new and unusual way, or he finds a way to invalidate them completely. Perhaps he decides to focus on the

---

[2] Kanagy, Conrad 2014 Survey of Credentialed Leaders in Mennonite Church USA

Scriptures that speak of God's love, while he rejects those that speak of God's judgments. Perhaps he only accepts the words of Jesus, as he rejects the words of Paul. Perhaps he decides that the God of Israel described in the Old Testament is a different God from the God revealed by Jesus Christ.

If homosexual activity is acceptable and good, then who is to say that other sexual activities that were formerly viewed as sinful are actually sinful? If homosexual sexual activity is acceptable, what is wrong with heterosexual, premarital sexual intercourse? Who really has the right to judge polygamy and other expressions of sexuality? People need to explore their sexuality, and try different things so that they can discover their true sexual identity.

The person who accepts gay marriage is very likely to accept the prevailing liberal view that gender is not determined by one's body parts. Just because you have male body parts does not mean you are a man. If you feel like a woman, you are in fact a woman, and everybody should celebrate that fact.

The person who believes that gay marriage is a holy, biblical institution is likely to question and eventually reject basic Christian doctrines. He is likely to doubt the existence of a literal eternal hell. He is likely to doubt whether Jesus is really the only way for men to receive eternal life. He is likely to believe that there are many paths to God, and that there are good things in all religions.

If you believe that there are many paths to God, and that all religions are basically good, why preach the Gospel? There is no hell, and who is to say that your views on eternal life are any better than someone else's? Who is to say that your religion is better than anyone else's?

A very radical change has taken place in the Mennonite Church. What was once considered evil is now praised as good. What was once considered unbiblical is now taught as biblical truth. Foundational doctrines of Christianity are being questioned and denied in the Mennonite colleges, universities, and seminaries. The educated elite of the Mennonite Church are radically changing their views on the foundational truths of Christianity.

DEEP DIVISIONS

The church is deeply, deeply divided. On the one side are the educated elite that dominate the seminaries, colleges, universities and denominational structures in the Mennonite church. This educated elite have radically changed views on sexuality, salvation, and the authority of Scripture.

On the other side are the more traditional, often working-class Mennonites who are trying to hold on to their communities, their religious traditions and the Scripture in a world that is increasingly hostile. These are deeply troubled by what is happening in the Mennonite educational institutions and church hierarchy. They are deeply troubled by the extreme changes that have taken place.

These two groups have less and less in common. Church split follows church split, as these two groups find it impossible to find a way to go forward in unity. Splits occur within conferences, as the more conservative churches decide they can no longer walk together with more liberal congregations.

MC USA was formed when two denominations, the (General Assembly) Mennonite Church and the General Conference Mennonite church merged in 2002 to form the Mennonite Church USA. Before the merger took place, the (General Assembly) Mennonite Church had approximately 69,000 members and the General Conference Mennonite church had approximately 64,000 members for a combined total of 133,000 members. In 2016, fourteen years after the merger, the combined Mennonite Church USA has 78,892 members. Church after church, district after district has been leaving.

In short, the Mennonite Church is in crisis. A church that prides itself in its "peace" position is tearing itself apart. Mennonites are unable to walk in unity with one another. The two sides cannot come together. The differences are simply too great.

The divisions in the Mennonite church are very, very deep. There is no easy way to reconcile a church in which half of the church is holding on to the traditional faith of its fathers, while the remainder of the church is turning away from every basic biblical doctrine.

In this book, we will look at what has happened to the Mennonite Church. Much of the Mennonite Church has been hijacked by the god of this world, the evil one himself. Instead of obeying the leading of the Holy spirit, it is obeying the leading of evil spirits.

As many of the religious systems of the Mennonite Church begin their final collapse, the Lord is calling forth his sons, those who hear His voice and do His will. "As many as are led by the Spirit of God, these are the sons of God." (Romans 8:14) He is raising up a people who do not follow religious traditions or deceptive spirits. They hear and obey the voice of the living God, and He uses them for His great works.

1 BLOOD COVENANTS

LEVELS OF EVIL

There are many sins that men commit. **"All of us have sinned, and fallen short of the glory of God."** (Romans 3:23) Why is homosexual sin different from any other sin? If the Mennonite Church accepts practicing homosexuals as members and leaders, why is that such a big deal?

Jesus taught that the man who lusts after a woman has already committed adultery with her in his heart. Which man has never committed the sin of lust? Which Mennonite leader has never lusted after a woman? If we accept these leaders, who have lusted after women, why shouldn't we accept leaders who are practicing homosexuals? Sin is sin, and we are all sinners.

Although all of us have sinned, there are still levels of sinfulness, levels of evil and perversion in the earth. In the Old Testament, we read of societies that became so evil and corrupted that God destroyed them completely. We read about the Amorites, who were deeply involved in sexual perversion, idol worship, and human sacrifice. When Abraham lived among the Amorites, he was told that the sin of the Amorites was not yet complete. When the sin of the Amorites was complete, they were destroyed by Abraham's descendants.

You can think of sin as an infection that begins in a small part of a person's body. If that infection is not healed, it spreads until gangrene and decay threatens the man's life. A man receives a small wound in his foot, which becomes infected. If the infection keeps spreading, the man's foot will begin to decay. The time comes when that man must amputate his foot to save his life.

In the same way, some societies become so decayed and corrupted that God must destroy them to save the rest of his creation on this earth. He does this out of mercy. It is more merciful for God to remove that society from the earth and bring its members before His judgment seat, than it is for Him to allow that society to spread its infection throughout the earth.

In the days before the flood, the entire earth became infected with sin to such a degree that **"the wickedness of men was great in the earth, and every intent of the thoughts of his heart was only evil continually."** (Genesis 6:5) As men hardened their hearts and completely rebelled against God, the time came when God needed to remove the decaying flesh from the earth and start over with Noah and his family.

In Genesis 19, we read the story of Sodom. The city of Sodom became so evil and corrupted, that the entire city became consumed with homosexual lust. When God sent His messengers to the city, the men of the city attempted to rape them. Abraham's nephew Lot gave the messengers shelter in his home as he tried to protect them from the evil intentions of his neighbors.

When the men of the city tried to invade Lot's home, Lot attempted to reason with them. He even offered to give them his own daughters if only they would leave the messengers of God alone. He pleaded with them **"Please, my brethren, do not do such a wicked deed!"**

The men of the city refused to listen to Lot. They accused Lot of judging them as they tried to break down his door so that they could rape the men inside. They said of Lot, **"This one came in to stay here, and he keeps acting as a judge; now we will deal worse with you than with them."**

They were struck with blindness, and the messengers of God warned Lot to flee from the city. When Lot left Sodom, the city was destroyed.

Sodom had become so evil, and so corrupted, that the only answer was destruction. When men completely set their hearts to doing evil, God releases destruction upon them. It was more merciful for God to destroy Sodom than to allow the sin to continue. If Sodom had been allowed to continue in its sin, it would have infected the whole earth with its rebellion and perversion. It is merciful to remove the cancer from a man's body instead of allowing it to continue growing.

Destruction is never God's first choice. Destruction only comes after God's messengers have been sent to a city. Abraham and Lot had testified to Sodom. Noah and Enoch had testified to the earth in the days before the flood. The Amorites had received the testimony of Abraham and Melchizedek.

Isaiah 5:20-21 states: **"Woe to those who call evil good, and good evil; Who put darkness for light, and light for darkness; Who put bitter for sweet, and sweet for bitter! Woe to those who are wise in their own eyes, And prudent in their own sight!"**

In the book of Jonah, we read about a city so evil that God was about to destroy it by fire. The spiritual darkness and confusion of this city was so great that men could not tell what was good from what was evil. They called evil good, and good evil. The Lord spoke about the moral confusion of this city, saying that they were **"unable to discern between their right hand and their left."** A light shone in this dark city, as Jonah warned them about the coming judgment. Nineveh repented and was saved from destruction.

In the prophecies of the last days found in the book of Revelation, we read about a people who will be so bitter and hardened against the Lord that they will refuse to repent even as God's judgments are released upon the earth. Terrible plagues will be released upon the entire earth in the last days, like the plagues that came upon Egypt. These plagues are God's final warning that complete destruction is coming. As the sun scorches men like fire (16:8), the rebels blasphemed the name of God and refused to repent. As darkness covers the earth and sores cover the bodies of men (16:2,3), the people gnaw their tongues in great pain and blaspheme the God of heaven.

As terrible hailstones weighting 75 pounds each fall upon the earth (16:21)and fire falls upon the earth the people blaspheme God and even form an army to try to attack God's people. In the end, these corrupt, rebellious, blasphemous nations are destroyed by the Lord and His army.

God sends his prophets and apostles to warn cities of His judgment. He warns cities that they are about to reap what they have sowed. Cities that have sowed sexual perversity, idolatry, and rebellion against the Lord will surely reap destruction. Cities that have sown bloodshed will surely reap bloodshed. This is the justice of God. Nations will reap what they have sown. This was true in Bible times, and it is true today.

TO WHOM MUCH IS GIVEN...MUCH IS REQUIRED

When men are completely committed to darkness, they call evil good, and good evil. They celebrate their evil deeds, as they accuse and condemn righteous men. When God sends His messengers to them, they accuse those messengers of trying to "judge" them, just as the Sodomites accused Lot. Finally, they reach a point in which the only answer to their deep iniquity is complete destruction. This was true in Bible times, and it is still true today.

It is important to know that God judges cities and nations according to the revelation and visitation that He has given to them. **"To whom much is given, much is required."** (Luke 12:48) Jesus said that on the Day of Judgment, Capernaum would be judged more severely than Sodom, and Bethsaida would be judged more severely than Tyre and Sidon. (Matt. 10:15) Certainly, Capernaum and Bethsaida seemed to be far more righteous that Sodom. However, Sodom only had the testimony of Lot, while Jesus himself preached the gospel of the kingdom and performed many miracles in Bethsaida and Capernaum. Therefore, they received a much more powerful testimony than Sodom had received. Lot was a righteous man, but he did not preach in the way that Jonah and Jesus preached. Therefore, Sodom will receive a lesser condemnation on the day of judgment.

To whom much is given, much is required. America has received more blessing from the Lord than almost any nation in history. The Spirit of God has been poured out upon America numerous times. There have been three great awakenings in America that brought much of the nation to faith in Christ. There have also been many other movements of the Holy Spirit in America, such as the Pentecostal movement that began on Azusa Street in Los Angeles in 1906, and the Charismatic renewal that took place in the 1970's. The written Word of God has been made easily available to every American.

What do you think happens when America turns its back on God and begins to celebrate evil? What do you think happens when America calls evil good, and good evil? The same condemnation that was released upon Capernaum and Bethsaida is released upon our nation.

We have received much. If there is not repentance, the great things that we have received from God will only increase the judgment that is released upon our nation.

CELEBRATING EVIL

The evil of homosexuality is found in the fact that many Christians are in the process of calling evil good, and good evil. It is one thing for people to commit evil deeds in secret, knowing that those deeds are evil as they hide in shame. It is a different level of evil when people bring those evil deeds into the public square and celebrate them. This is happening in America. Homosexual sin is being celebrated in the public square. The men of Sodom united together in the public square, unashamed as they attempted to force their perversion upon the servants of God. In the same way, homosexual sin is being celebrated in the public square of every major city in America.

BRINGING BAAL INTO THE TEMPLE

It might be helpful to compare the sin of homosexuality to idol worship.

In Old Testament times, men worshipped Baal. They built their altars on mountainsides, in places that seemed to be special or "spiritual".

These altars were called high places in the Bible. At those altars, sacrifices were made before the idols of Baal. Those who worshipped Baal at these altars were guilty of great evil.

Those who brought the idols of Baal into the temple of the Lord were guilty of a much greater evil. During the days of Manasseh, the worship of false gods was brought right into the temple of God. A carved image of Ashura was set up inside the temple. Altars to various false gods were erected inside the temple. The place where God said, "I will put my name" (II Kings 21:4) became a place where evil spirits were worshiped.

This idolatry inside the temple of God stirred the jealousy of God more than all the idolatry that was committed before those times. The Lord spoke a terrible judgment through his prophets regarding His chosen city, over Jerusalem and the temple itself. He said "**'So this is what the LORD, the God of Israel, says: I will bring such disaster on Jerusalem and Judah that the ears of those who hear about it will tingle with horror...I will wipe away the people of Jerusalem as one wipes a dish and turns it upside down. Then I will reject even the remnant of my own people who are left, and I will hand them over as plunder for their enemies. For they have done great evil in my sight and have angered me ever since their ancestors came out of Egypt.**" (II Kings 21: 13-15)

God kept His promise. In 597 BC, on a terrible day of darkness and death, the army of the Babylonians defeated the army of Judah. In 586 BC, the Babylonian army completely destroyed Jerusalem. The Babylonian soldiers of King Nebuchadnezzar burned the house of God, broke down the wall of Jerusalem, burned all its palaces with fire and destroyed all its precious possessions (2 Chronicles 36:20). The Jews were slaughtered like cattle and the survivors were sold into slavery in Babylon.

Which is worse, to worship Baal under a tree on the mountainside, or to bring the idol of Baal inside the temple of God to worship him in the temple? It is an evil thing when men perform evil deeds in secret.

It is a much worse evil when men bring their evil deeds inside the temple of God and claim that their evil is sanctioned by God.

The man who places God's name upon evil is very guilty. If you must sin, at least keep God's name out of it. If you place God's name upon your sin, you are adding the sin of blasphemy to your original sin.

This is the great evil that is found in Chester Wenger's letter. When two men have sexual intercourse in shame and in secret, it is an evil thing. When those same two men bring their sin into the "temple" and claim that they are participating in a holy covenant blessed by God, it represents a much greater evil.

Wenger makes it very clear in his letter that homosexuals should not be forced to conduct their love affairs outside the church. Their sexuality should not be "left to fend for itself outside the church." Homosexuals should bring their sexual relationships inside the church. They should enter holy, homosexual marriages inside the church, that are blessed and accountable to the church.

When two men do this, they are adding the sin of blasphemy to their sexual sin. When you bring something that is unholy into the church and declare that it is holy, you are not causing that thing to be holy! You are only adding the sin of blasphemy to your original sin. When Wenger says that the "light of Christ" is leading him to celebrate homosexual relationships, he is deeply, deeply deceived. He is not listening to the Spirit of Christ. He is obeying another spirit entirely.

JESUS DIDN'T DIE SO THAT WE CAN CONTINUE TO SIN

The Holy Spirit is holy. The Holy Spirit never makes excuses for men's sins. The Holy Spirit leads us to repentance so that we can be freed from the power of sin. The power of the Cross never gives men excuses to continue living in sin. The power of the Cross is there to deliver men from sin.

There is no excuse for sexual sin! There is no excuse for the man who remains trapped in lust, masturbation and pornography! There is an open door for those who want to leave these sins, but there is no excuse or grace for those who decide to remain in them!

One of the greatest lies of our time is that the slavery of sin must continue even after a man turns to Christ. It is assumed that Christians will continue to obey their lust, even after they have made a commitment to Christ.

This is a lie from hell. All through the New Testament we read about the bondage of sin and deliverance from sin. Never do we read excuses for those who would choose to continue in sin after they have received forgiveness for sin. On the contrary, some of the greatest warnings in Scripture are reserved for those who would claim to follow Christ and yet continue in their sins.

Peter speaks of those who have escaped the corruption of sin, and then are lured back into the lusts of the flesh:

> **For if, after they have escaped the pollutions of the world through the knowledge of the Lord and Savior Jesus Christ, they are again entangled in them and overcome, the latter end is worse for them than the beginning. For it would have been better for them not to have known the way of righteousness, than having known it, to turn from the holy commandment delivered to them. But it has happened to them according to the true proverb: "A dog returns to his own vomit," and, "And the sow, having washed, to her wallowing in the mire " (II Peter 2:20-22).**

Peter is saying that it would be better for someone never to have known the forgiveness of sins that is in Christ, than to have known that forgiveness, and turned back to sin. This is a severe warning. The power of Christ and the forgiveness of Christ are available to change us. They are available to transform us. The blood of Jesus Christ cleanses us from all sin. This includes homosexual sin and every other form of sexual sin. However, we must change! We are not free to continue living in sin after we have turned to Christ.

It is a great evil to say that because Jesus died for me and forgave my sin, I can continue sinning! The one who lives life in this way will end up in a worse condition than the one who never turned to Jesus. If you are overcome by sin and continue living in sexual sin, you are terribly lost.

This terrible warning is found in the Word of God, not the word of man. If you continue living in sexual sin, after you have confessed Christ, you are lost. This is just as true for the man who lives his life in bondage to pornography and masturbation, as it is for the homosexual who claims that God made him that way and therefore he is free to continue sinning.

Perhaps the greatest deception of our time is to say that God himself has made us the way we are, and therefore we are not responsible for our sin. This is adding the sin of blasphemy to the sin, blaming God for our evil actions.

MARRIAGE IS A BLOOD COVENANT
To understand sexual sin, it is necessary to understand the biblical teachings on blood covenant. The first mention of blood covenant is found in Genesis 2.

Jesus quoted these verses as he discussed the sanctity of marriage and the evil of divorce with the Pharisees: **"For this reason a man shall leave his father and mother and be joined to his wife, and the two shall become one flesh. So then, they are no longer two but one flesh. Therefore, what God has joined together, let not man separate."**

The simplest definition of blood covenant is found in these words: "And the two shall become one flesh." In blood covenant, two become one.

Marriage is a form of blood covenant. When a man leaves his father and mother and is united with his wife, the two become one flesh. They form a covenant together, a blood covenant. The female body is created in such a way, that when a woman has sexual intercourse for the first time, there is blood. God created the body this way to show that sexual intercourse is a holy covenant, a blood covenant joining a man and woman together for life.

This holy covenant is God's idea. Marriage did not originate in the mind of man. God saw the loneliness of Adam and said, **"It is not good that man should be alone; I will make him a helper**

comparable to him (Genesis 2:18)." Marriage is God's idea, just as gender is God's idea.

In the covenant of marriage, two become one. If my wife finds my wallet and "borrows" 100 dollars, can I call the police and report the theft of my money? Of course not. The money in my wallet belongs to her. Everything I have belongs to her, and everything she has belongs to me. We are one.

This is God's original intention for the marriage covenant. In marriage, two become one. A husband and wife share their bodies, their possessions, and their lives together.

Marriage has a price. Marriage is not easy. Marriage is not only honeymoon. It is a blood covenant. A blood covenant costs you your life.

In marriage, a man does not simply obey his lust. Rather, he refuses to be controlled by his lust. He kills his desire for other women. He gives himself completely to his wife and his family. Every day, a married man goes to work and labors for the sake of his family. Every day, he kills his desire to live for himself and lives for his family instead.

In the same way, a mother pays a high price in marriage. Every day she labors for her husband and her children. She clothes them and feeds them. She refuses to follow the lust of her flesh. She serves her family, and she serves her husband.

In some ways, marriage is a form of dying. A husband and a wife die to their selfish desires, as they lay down their lives for one another and serve one another. And as they die, life comes. A family is born.

There is great blessing in this plan. There is relationship. There is life and love and family in this plan. There is sexual intercourse in this plan between a man and a woman who are committed to one another for life. Marriage is created by God for intimacy, pleasure, and life between these who are joined in lifelong covenant with one another.

Blood covenant releases the greatest blessings that mankind can receive. Just as a blood covenant is at the foundation of life and family, blood covenant is at the center of our salvation.

At the very center of Christianity there is a blood covenant, formed between God and man through the blood of Jesus Christ. Jesus Christ gave his blood for us, so that we can enter into a new covenant with the living God. This blood covenant is the result of God's extreme love for us, as He gave everything He had for us.

This covenant cost God everything. If you completely give yourself to this covenant, it will also cost you everything. Jesus said **"…He who does not take his cross and follow after me is not worthy of me. He who finds his life will lose it, and he who loses his life for My sake will find it."**(Matt. 10:38,39)

THE DOMINION OF THE EVIL ONE THROUGH COVENANT

God uses blood covenant to release His greatest blessings upon the earth. But just as a blood covenant is used for great good, it can also be used for great evil. The devil uses blood covenant to release great evil upon the earth.

The devil came to Jesus and showed him all the kingdoms of the world in a moment of time. He said to Jesus, **"All this authority I will give You, and their glory; for this has been delivered to me, and I give it to whomever I wish. Therefore, if you will worship before me, all will be yours (Luke 4:6-7)."**

The devil told Jesus that all the kingdoms of men had been given to him, and that he could give them to whomever he wished. On this point, the devil was telling the truth. The kingdoms of the world have been given to the devil.

Who gave these kingdoms to the devil? Certainly God did not give these kingdoms to the devil. When God created the earth, he created man to have dominion over the earth. He said, **"Let Us make man in Our image, according to Our likeness; let them have dominion over the fish of the sea, over the birds of the air, and over the**

cattle, over all the earth and over every creeping thing that creeps on the earth (Genesis 1:26)."

Psalm 115:16 says, **"The heaven, even the heavens, are the LORD's; But the earth He has given to the children of men."**

To a large degree, the earth has been given into the hands of men. Although people love to blame God for every bad thing that happens in this world, the atrocities that take place on the earth usually take place because people have allowed them to happen or caused them to happen. The terrible suffering that takes place on the earth is a direct result of people's choices. When man rebelled against God, suffering and death entered this world.

If God created man to have dominion over the earth, how then did the devil take possession over the kingdoms of this world?

The devil understands the power of a blood covenant. The devil knows that if he can deceive a man into forming a blood covenant with him, everything that man has will belong to the devil. In covenant, two become one. In covenant, everything that was given to man is given into the hands of the evil one. In covenant, all the authority that God gave to man over the earth is turned over to the devil. The devil is very, very skillful at deceiving people into forming covenants with him.

BLOOD COVENANTS WITH BAAL

When you read the Old Testament, you read about temples that were built to worship Baal. When a man wished to worship Baal, he went to the temple of Baal. Great feasts were held in the temple of Baal. Goats and other animals would be sacrificed to Baal. Then everyone would eat the meat of those goats in the feasts that were held in Baal's temple. As the people ate the meat of those goats, what were they doing? They were forming a blood covenant between themselves and Baal. In a blood covenant, two become one. As they ate the meat of that goat, the people gave themselves to Baal. They became the people of Baal. He became their god, and they became his people.

In the temple of Baal, there were not only idols. There were also prostitutes in the temple of Baal. When a man wanted to worship Baal, he went to the temple of Baal and had sexual relations with the temple prostitute.

Why were there prostitutes in the temple of Baal? Because of blood covenant. These temple prostitutes were the representatives of Baal. When a man slept with the prostitute who was dedicated to Baal, he formed a blood covenant between himself and Baal.

In this way men were deceived into forming covenants with the devil. As they attended the feasts that were held at the temple of Baal and slept with the prostitutes who were dedicated to Baal, they formed blood covenants with the false god Baal. Baal, of course, is the representative of the devil himself.

BALAAM AND ISRAEL'S COVENANT WITH BAAL

In Numbers 22-26 we read the story of Balaam that teaches us about covenant. Balaam was a sorcerer, honored and feared by many. The Moabites heard the stories of the Israelite nation that was marching toward them. They heard about Israel's deliverance from Egypt. They heard about the terrible plagues that were released upon Egypt, and the parting of the Red Sea.

The Moabites turned to the greatest sorcerer of their region, Balaam, and asked him to come and curse the Israelites for them. Although Balaam was a sorcerer, he had some knowledge of God. To some degree he feared God. The king of the Moabites, Balak, sent his men with money to pay Balaam to curse Israel. Balaam inquired of the Lord, and the Lord warned him not to curse Israel. The Moabite leaders came a second time, and Balaam inquired of the Lord again what he should do. The Lord told him to go with them, but only to speak what He told him to speak.

As Balaam traveled to the place where he was expected to curse Israel, his donkey refused to go forward. Balaam's donkey saw an angel with a sword standing in the path, ready to slay Balaam. After beating his donkey, the donkey's mouth was opened, and Balaam's eyes were opened. He saw the angel with a sword, ready to slay him. Once again Balaam was warned to only speak what God told him to speak. And so, Balaam continued in the fear of the Lord. He knew that if he added to God's words, he would be killed.

When it came time to curse Israel, seven altars were prepared on the high places of Baal, and animals were sacrificed on the altars. Instead of cursing Israel, Balaam blessed Israel and cursed her enemies. Balaam prophesied: **"How shall I curse whom God has not cursed? And how shall I denounce whom the LORD has not denounced?"**

When Balak took Balaam to a different location to curse Israel, Balaam rebuked Balak with the word of the Lord: "**Rise up, Balak, and hear! Listen to me, son of Zippor! 'God is not a man, that He should lie, Nor a son of man, that He should repent….' Behold, I have received a command to bless; He has blessed, and I cannot reverse it…. For there is no sorcery against Jacob, Nor any divination against Israel."** Balaam ended his prophecies with a proclamation about the coming Messiah.

Balaam did not sin in the prophecies that he spoke which are recorded in Numbers. And yet in the book of Revelation Jesus speaks about Balaam in a very negative way. He says that Balaam **"taught Balak to put a stumbling block before the children of Israel, to eat things sacrificed to idols, and to commit sexual immorality."** (Revelation 2:14)

Evidently, Balaam committed a great sin that is not recorded in the book of Numbers. After blessing Israel instead of cursing Israel, King Balak was furious with Balaam. Balaam didn't want Balak to be angry with him, so he told Balak: "I cannot curse Israel. God has warned me that if I speak any word against Israel, I will be killed. However, if you want to defeat Israel, I can tell you how to do it. If you want to defeat Israel, you must form a blood covenant with Israel. If you form a blood covenant with Israel, you can stop them. Tell your women to dress in their best clothing. Send them down to the camp of the

Israelites, so that they can seduce the men of Israel. Tell them to sleep with the men of Israel, and to invite them to a feast in the temple of Baal. In this way, you will form a covenant with Israel, and they will come under the judgment of their God."

In Numbers 25, after Balaam had left Balak, we read the following:

> **Now Israel remained in Acacia Grove, and the people began to commit harlotry with the women of Moab. They invited the people to the sacrifices of their Gods, and the people ate and bowed down to their Gods. So, Israel was joined to Baal of Peor, and the anger of the LORD was aroused against Israel** (Numbers 25:1-3).

In this verse, we see the results of Balaam's evil advice. King Balak sent the Moabite women into the camp of Israel. They committed sexual immorality with the men of Israel, and invited the Israelites to their ceremonies of Baal worship. Animal sacrifices were made to Baal, and the men of Israel ate those sacrifices. As they ate the meat of animals offered to Baal, and committed sexual immorality with the women of Moab, they formed blood covenants.

In these covenants, the men of Israel were not only connected to the women of Midian. The Bible says, "So Israel was joined to Baal." As the men committed sexual immorality with the Moabite women, they formed a blood covenant with Baal. As the men ate the meat of animals offered to Baal, they formed a blood covenant with Baal.

Balaam had prophesied judgment upon Moab. He said, **"A Scepter shall rise out of Israel, and batter the brow of Moab, and destroy all the sons of tumult."** Now Israel was joined to Moab in blood covenants with the women of Moab and with Baal.

Because Israel was joined to Moab and to Baal in covenant, Israel needed to share in the judgment that God intended to be released upon Moab. Judgment begins in the house of the Lord. (I Peter 4:17) Israel needed to be judged before Moab was judged.

And so, the anger of the Lord was aroused against Israel. The judgment of God that should have come upon Moab came upon Israel instead. God released a terrible plague against Israel, and 24,000 Israelites were killed in the plague.

SEXUAL IMMORALITY AND BLOOD COVENANT

Do you understand why there are so many warnings in the Bible about sexual immorality? When the men of Israel slept with the Moabite women, they were not only joined to those women, but they were also joined to the god of those women. They were joined to Baal. When you sleep with someone, you sleep with that person and that person's demons.

In Proverbs 5, the writer warns a young man not to be seduced by an adulterous woman. He warns that the adulterous woman will lead the young man to hell. Why does he speak in this way? When you commit adultery, you are joining yourself to your partner in immorality. You become connected to that person . If the person is on a road to hell, he/she will take you along also.

The man who makes a covenant with the devil will share in the devil's judgment. God created a lake of fire in which the devil and his angels will be thrown. The one who makes a covenant with the devil is connected to the devil, and he will be thrown into the same lake of fire.

He who overcomes shall inherit all things, and I will be his God and he shall be My son. But the cowardly, unbelieving, abominable, murderers, sexually immoral, sorcerers, idolaters, and all liars shall have their part in the lake which burns with fire and brimstone, which is the second death (Revelation 21:7-8).

Who are the sexually immoral, the sorcerers, and idolaters? Are they not those who form blood covenants with evil spirits? The one who forms covenants with evil spirits will share in their judgment.

1 Corinthians 3:15-17 says: **"If anyone's work is burned, he will suffer loss; but he himself will be saved, yet so as through fire. Do you not know that you are the temple of God and that the Spirit of God dwells in you? If anyone defiles the temple of God,**

26

God will destroy him. For the temple of God is holy, which temple you are. "

THE EARLY CHURCH FORBADE EVIL COVENANTS

In Acts 15 we read about a dispute that took place in the early church. Gentiles were turning to the Lord, and putting their faith in Jesus Christ. Some of the Jews demanded that these Gentile believers be circumcised and obey the law of Moses. The disagreement became so intense, that Paul, Barnabas, and others were sent to Jerusalem to bring the issue before the apostles. In Jerusalem, the apostles decided that Gentile believers did not need to follow the law of Moses. They were free to obey the Spirit of God, as He led them. Only four things were asked of the Gentile believers. They were asked to abstain from meat offered to idols, from meat that was strangled, from blood, and from sexual immorality.

Why did the apostles ask the Gentile believers to abstain from these things? Each of these things is related to blood covenant. When an animal is sacrificed before an idol, those who eat that meat form a blood covenant with the spirits that are connected to that idol. Likewise, the Gentile believers were asked to abstain from eating blood or meat that still had an animal's blood in it (animals that were strangled). Finally, they were asked to abstain from sexual immorality. Sexual immorality is a form of blood covenant.

In other words, Gentile believers were freed from the law of Moses, but they were forbidden to form evil covenants! And today, believers are free to obey the Holy Spirit as He leads. However, the Lord will never lead you into evil covenants. He will never lead you to commit sexual immorality. He will never lead you into covenants with evil spirits. These things are an abomination to the Lord.

These evil covenants cannot be made holy. In fact, they are covenants with the powers of darkness. When a man participates in these covenants, he is declaring that he belongs to the evil spirits who are part of these covenants.

This is why sexual sin is such a serious issue. This is why the enemy is trying to fill our nation, our culture, and our churches with sexual sin. It is impossible to walk with the Lord as we form covenants with darkness. It is impossible to obey the Lord while committing sexual immorality.

HOMOSEXUAL SIN

Homosexual sin is an advanced form of sexual immorality. The body of a Christian is called the temple of God. The one who defiles God's temple through sexual immorality will be destroyed by God (I Corinthians 3:17). Consider the following scriptures that speak of homosexuality and other forms of sexual sin, and the consequences of unrepented sin:

> **For this reason God gave them up to vile passions. For even their women exchanged the natural use for what is against nature.**

> **Likewise also the men, leaving the natural use of the woman, burned in their lust for one another, men with men committing what is shameful, and receiving in themselves the penalty of their error which was due (Romans 1:26-27).**

> **As Sodom and Gomorrah, and the cities around them in a similar manner to these, having given themselves over to sexual immorality and gone after strange flesh, are set forth as an example, suffering the vengeance of eternal fire (Jude 1:7).**

> **Do you not know that the unrighteous will not inherit the kingdom of God? Do not be deceived. Neither fornicators, nor idolaters, nor adulterers, nor homosexuals, nor sodomites, nor thieves, nor covetous, nor drunkards, nor revilers, nor extortioners will inherit the kingdom of God (1 Corinthians 6:9-10).**

> **Flee sexual immorality. Every sin that a man does is outside the body, but he who commits sexual immorality sins against his own body.**

Or do you not know that your body is the temple of the Holy Spirit who is in you, whom you have from God, and you are not your own? (1 Corinthians 6:18-19)

Do you not know that you are the temple of God and that the Spirit of God dwells in you?

If anyone defiles the temple of God, God will destroy him. For the temple of God is holy, which temple you are (1 Corinthians 3:16-17).

Marriage is honorable among all, and the bed undefiled; but fornicators and adulterers God will judge (Hebrews 13:4).

ARE GAYS BORN THAT WAY?

In America today, most people think that gays and lesbians are "born that way". In a recent Gallup poll, 51 percent of the respondents believed that people are born gay or lesbian. They think that genetics determines whether someone is heterosexual or homosexual.[3]

Recent scientific studies have conclusively proven that homosexuality is not determined by a person's genetic makeup. These studies have examined the sexual preferences of identical twins. Identical twins share identical DNA with each other. If homosexuality were determined by a person's genetic makeup, then if one identical twin were homosexual, the other should also be homosexual.

This rarely happens. In one study conducted by Peter Bearman and Hannah Bruckner of Columbia and Yale University, when one male identical twin was a homosexual, the other twin shared his homosexual identity only 7.7 percent of the time. Likewise, when a female twin identified herself as homosexual, her twin shared her homosexual identity only 5.3 percent of the time. [4]

---

[3] www.gallup.com/poll/183332/majority-say-gays-lesbians-born-not-made.aspx
[4] https://pdfs.semanticscholar.org/112f/8e9c215945b50e953394346c652e301d6828.pdf

There have been seven other major studies of identical twins during the last two decades. They all came to the same conclusion as Bearman and Bruckner's study: homosexuality is not determined by one's genetics. There is no gay gene.

HOMOSEXUALITY AND CIVIL RIGHTS

If there is no gay gene, then why do most people think that gays are "born that way"? Quite simply, homosexual activists want homosexual rights to be treated as a civil rights issue. They do not want homosexual activity to be viewed as a choice, or a sin. They want to it to be treated just like race. It is impossible for a person to change his/her race, and they want homosexuality to be viewed the same way.

Gay activists want to force churches to hire homosexuals to work in their schools and congregations. They want to force Christian businessmen to hire gays to work in their businesses. They want to turn elementary schools into centers of homosexual propaganda, where gay identity and lifestyle are celebrated.

Their goal is not merely to force Christian businesses to serve homosexuals. They want to force Christian businessmen to participate in gay weddings and gay pride parades. Most Christian businessmen would happily serve homosexuals in most areas of business, but they do not want to be forced to participate in ceremonies and celebrations that they believe are evil.

To accomplish these goals, homosexual activists must treat those who are morally opposed to their activities as racists. They want to make opposition to the gay agenda as reprehensible as racism in American society. A racist is unlikely to be hired by America's corporations, schools, or government agencies. If even a hint of racism can be proven in these settings, lawsuits are filed and large settlements are awarded to the aggrieved parties. Because of these lawsuits, companies and other organizations are very careful not to hire racists.

Gay activists want to make it nearly impossible for committed Christians to hold jobs in these same settings. They want to file lawsuits against any Christian who believes that homosexual activity is a sin. They want to drive Christians out of the public sphere, out of corporations, and even out of their own small businesses. This is already happening.

The truth is, homosexuals are not born that way. The studies on identical twins show that many people who experienced same sex attraction during one part of their life change their sexual attraction in a later stage of life. Most teenagers who experience same sex attractions later become fully committed to a heterosexual lifestyle. These changes take place without counseling or therapy. Homosexual attraction and identity is not something that is completely fixed from birth. [5]

FAMILY BREAKDOWN AND HOMOSEXUALITY

If sexual orientation is not determined by a person's genetics, then what causes a person to be sexually attracted to members of the same sex? Researchers Bearman and Brueckner concluded that the way children were raised had a great effect on their sexual orientation. They concluded that "less gendered socialization in early childhood and preadolescence shapes subsequent same-sex romantic preferences."

What does "less gendered socialization" mean? In simplified terms, it means that a boy grew up without a positive relationship with a father figure. He lacked a positive male role model. He grew up yearning for male love and attention. It means that a girl grew up without a positive relationship with a mother. She lacked a positive mother figure. She grew up yearning for female love and attention.

Of course, not every child who grows up in these circumstances turns out to be gay. However, a significant percentage do.

In fact, the spread of homosexuality through American society is connected to the breakdown of the family. When two selfish people refuse to serve one another in marriage, they usually begin to tear one another down and eventually destroy the relationship. This usually ends in divorce.

---

[5] emedicine.medscape.com/article/917792-overview

In divorce, a blood covenant is broken. Souls that have become one are ripped apart. The pain and suffering caused by broken marriage covenants are intense. The children of divorce suffer the most. The family that God intended for them to have is torn away from them. Millions of young men and women grow up without the relationship with a father (or mother) that God intended them to have.

The children of divorce grow up with gaping wounds in their souls. Many go from sexual relationship to sexual relationship as they try to fill the holes in their soul. Some boys who lacked a healthy relationship with their father feel an intense craving for a close relationship with a man. Some become involved in homosexual relationships as they try to satisfy this craving.

Meanwhile, young girls who grow up without a father also try to fill the emotional holes in their lives. As they grow older, they crave male love and attention, and they are willing to give sex to get it. Shallow and manipulative men learn how to play these young women to get what they want.

HOMOSEXUALITY AND SEXUAL ABUSE

As already mentioned, sexual intercourse is a form of blood covenant. In a blood covenant, two become one. In marriage, this is a positive force as two people are connected to build a family together. The enemy uses the connections formed by sexual immorality to wound people as those covenants are broken and to connect people to the wrong people and to evil spirits.

The most destructive form of sexual immorality is found in child molestation and abuse. A large percentage of practicing homosexuals were sexually abused as children. One study found that 46 percent of homosexual men had been sexually molested by men during their boyhood.[6] If you consider that some homosexual men in the study

---

[6] Marie, E. Tomeo, et al., "Comparative Data of Childhood and Adolescence Molestation in Heterosexual and Homosexual Persons," Archives of Sexual Behavior 30 (2001): 539.

probably hid the abuse that they suffered, the actual number of those who were abused is probably higher.

Sexual intercourse connects two people together. When sexual abuse takes place, a certain kind of emotional and spiritual tie is formed between the child and his abuser. The enemy uses this connection to influence the child's life. He uses this connection to confuse the child's sexual identity and orientation.

This seems very cruel and unfair. The child is innocent, and yet his life becomes twisted and perverted because of the actions of another. But, in fact, this is the way that sin always works. Sin always affects those around us. If a man commits adultery, his sin doesn't only affect himself. The man's sin affects his wife and his children. They suffer greatly because of what he did.

In the same way, child abuse releases a kind of spiritual infection that eats away at the life of the child. The child is connected to his abuser because of the covenantal nature of sexual sin. In time, the enemy might be able to warp the life of that child to such a high degree that the child becomes an abuser himself when he grows up.

SEDUCED INTO HOMOSEXUALITY

There is a third reason why people become involved in homosexual behavior. Some are simply seduced into homosexuality. Everyone wants to be loved.

Some homosexuals experience strong same sex attraction from a very early age. Others do not experience this attraction, and yet they enter a homosexual lifestyle.

Some people are seduced into the homosexual lifestyle. They don't grow up feeling attracted to members of the same sex, but they decide to experiment with a homosexual relationship anyway. This often takes place on college campuses.

Radical feminists dominate certain fields of study in American academia, such as women's studies, literature, and sociology. A significant portion of these scholars are likely to be lesbians. A female who is taught by these professors is likely to be deeply influenced by their views on sexuality. These feminists constantly expound on the evils of patriarchy. They teach young women that heterosexual marriages are oppressive. They encourage young women to explore their sexual identities.

And so, the young woman listens to her teacher and begins to experiment with lesbian relationships. Although she never experienced same sex attraction as a girl, she decides to experiment with a lesbian relationship. The people whom she looks up to in college are all encouraging her to do so, and she acquiesces.

Once this young woman begins a lesbian relationship, the hook is set. Sexual intercourse is a form of blood covenant. The woman is now connected to her lesbian lover, and to the evil spirits that are part of her lover's life.

Some of these women come back to their senses after they leave the academic environment. They marry men and raise children. Others go deeper into the lesbian lifestyle.

Likewise, young men who are involved in fields dominated by homosexuals can also be seduced into a homosexual relationship. A young man who loves theater might find himself surrounded by homosexuals. The people he likes and admires are homosexuals. Perhaps this young man never felt very confident in his masculinity. Perhaps he was very artistic in nature and not very good at sports and other "masculine" activities. Although that young man never felt attracted to men in his boyhood, he might be seduced into a homosexual relationship as he becomes a young adult. He might actually feel socially ostracized if he doesn't become involved in homosexuality. When someone he likes and admires pursues him, he might decide to experiment with a homosexual relationship. Once he has intercourse with a man, the hook is set. He has formed a blood covenant with that man, a connection that is difficult to break.

In these ways, homosexual sin spreads through a society. Homosexuals are not five or ten percent of a population that have homosexual DNA. Homosexuals are the product of the sin of a society. They are the product of the broken homes, evil sexual covenants, and sinful choices. In many cases, they are the result of sexual abuse.

Just as ten percent of a population is not "born" gay, the percentage of homosexuals in a population is not limited to ten percent. Homosexuality can spread like an infection through a population. As the families break down, more and more children are emotionally wounded because they lack a good relationship with their father or mother. These emotional wounds open the door for homosexuality to spread. Likewise, as the family breaks down, children become more susceptible to sexual abuse. When a father is not present to protect the children, the children can become easier prey for sexual predators. The child that has been sexually abused is far more likely to become a homosexual or even a sexual abuser himself.

THE CORRUPTION OF ENTIRE SOCIETIES

In some societies, homosexuality has spread to such a degree that the majority of adult males participate in homosexual relationships. This can be seen in the Pashtun ethnic group that is found in Afghanistan and northern Pakistan. The Pashtuns are a large tribe, with almost 14 million members in Afghanistan and more than 30 million members in Pakistan.

Many Pashtun men participate in a form of child molestation known as bacha bazi. Bacha bazi is a traditional practice in which young boys become the possession of older men. Sometimes these boys are bought from their parents. In other cases, they are simply kidnapped. The boys are known as the beardless ones, and they take the passive or female role in the relationship.

Pashtun men take pride in their boys. They hold parties in which the boys dance and show off their charms. At the end of the dance, the boys are taken home by the men.

Bacha bazi is so pervasive in Pashtun society that it is estimated that half of all Pashtun men participate in the practice. Boys become bacha bazis at the age of 12-15 years. They become the sexual playthings of older men until they reach the age at which they start looking for boys of their own.

Bacha bazi would seem to be in direct contradiction to Islamic theology. Some forms of Shariah law demand the execution of homosexuals. However, most adult men who own boys would deny that they are in fact homosexuals. They interpret the Islamic laws against homosexuality to apply only to those who actually fall in love with members of the same sex. Because they are only using these boys as playthings, they are not homosexuals.

American and British soldiers have often been horrified by what they discovered in Afghanistan. In some cases, the Americans pushed out the Taliban, only to discover that the Afghanis who replaced them were even worse. They discovered that some of the Afghani soldiers and administrators that they worked with were actually child molesters who kidnapped and raped young men.

One group of British Royal Marines was shocked when they went on patrol in a remote Pashtun village. They were surrounded by homosexual men trying to proposition them. "It was hell," said Corporal Paul Richard. "Every village we went into we got a group of men wearing make-up coming up, stroking our hair and cheeks and making kissing noises."[7]

The practice of bacha bazi has twisted and perverted Pashtun society, including its view of women. The men who participate in bacha bazi often show great disdain for women. Women are considered to be unclean because of their monthly periods. A common saying in Pashtun society is "women for marriage, boys for pleasure."

Pashtun society is a very traditional religious society. Nonetheless, sexual perversion has permeated the tribe to a degree that San Francisco, California, seems like a very moral place by comparison. Religion is not the answer to sexual perversion and lawlessness.

---

[7] Stephen, Chris (5/24/02) Startled UK Marines Hassled by Gay Afghans, TheScotsman.net

Homosexual activists become enraged if anyone suggests that there is a connection between homosexuality and child molestation. Nevertheless, the connection is there. Many homosexuals were sexually abused as children. Many homosexual men are sexually attracted to adolescent males, and many adolescent males who come from broken homes are eager to develop a close relationship with an older male. The young teenager who walks into a gay bar for the first time will likely find no shortage of older men who desire to "mentor" him into a homosexual lifestyle.

The SIGMA Project (1992) interviewed and followed almost a thousand homosexuals in Britain over a three-year period and found that "50 percent of homosexuals had their first same-sex experience with an adult by the age of 14." The age of consent in Great Britain is 16.

THE CORRUPTION OF AMERICA

America is headed down a very dark road. Sexual sin is spreading through society to an incredible degree. Sins that were once considered repulsive and shameful are now celebrated in the streets. Politicians and society's leaders fall over themselves as they try to express their deep and unwavering support for the homosexual community and its activities. Teachers in elementary and middle schools try to identify children who might have homosexual tendencies so that they can help those children make choices that will result in their taking on a homosexual identity.

And in the church, Christian schools and universities are churning out thousands of graduates who are deeply convinced that gay marriage is a holy institution and that God has created people to be gay. As these graduates gain positions of authority in church institutions, the church slides into apostasy. This is happening in many Christian denominations at this very moment.

VAUGHN MARTIN

2 TWO RELIGIONS

MENNONITE COLLEGES CHOOSE GAY MARRIAGE

In 2015, the United States Supreme Court ruled in Obergefell v. Hodges that the Constitution of the United States guarantees a fundamental right to marry for same sex couples. All state level bans on same sex marriage were therefore overruled.

This ruling created a quandary for The Council for Christian Colleges and Universities (CCCU), which represented 118 schools in the United States, most of which tried to uphold traditional Christian teachings on sexuality and marriage. Many school administrators feared that if their institutions remained faithful to Christian teachings on sexuality and marriage, they could be sued for having discriminatory practices.

Two Mennonite schools in the CCCU, Eastern Mennonite University and Goshen College, used the Supreme Court ruling as an opportunity to make their beliefs clear to the world. They immediately added "sexual orientation" to their nondiscrimination policies and declared their willingness to hire staff and faculty who are part of same-sex marriages. When it became clear that their change in policies would bring conflict with other members of the CCCU, both schools withdrew their membership from the organization that they had helped to found.

John Brenneman, president of Goshen College, released a statement explaining the change: "We seek forbearance and grace amidst our differences. We deeply affirm the goodness of marriage, singleness, celibacy, sexual intimacy within marriage, and a life of faithfulness before God for all people," wrote Brenneman. He declared that unmarried employees of the school would be expected to remain celibate. With these words, Brenneman followed the example of Chester Wenger. He used good and spiritual words to describe Goshen College's embrace of gay marriage.

How did the Mennonite church arrive at this point? These leaders, whether conservative or liberal, all sound so committed to doing what is right. They all seem like such committed Christians. They all talk about following Christ.

Anabaptists in general emphasize the importance of not only believing in Christ but actually following Him in one's daily life. Anabaptist theologians often draw a distinction between Anabaptist theology and evangelical theology. Evangelicals emphasize faith, simply believing in what Christ has done; Anabaptists emphasize the fact that Christians must actually follow Jesus in day to day life. They must not only believe in Christ. They must also take up their cross and follow after Him. Conservative and liberal Anabaptists believe this and preach this.

TWO RELIGIONS

Although the words are similar, it is difficult to imagine two groups that are farther apart than liberal Mennonites and conservative Mennonites. If you compare a conservative Mennonite farming community to one of the liberal, educated, middle class Mennonite communities that forms around a Mennonite college, they would seem to have very little in common. Although both groups come from the same root system, they have moved very far apart indeed.

In fact, two very different religions have formed, both using the name "Mennonite". These two religions have some similarities with each other, but they also have deep differences. Both religions value "peace" and "community", and yet those words mean very different things for each group. Both groups seem to be very committed to their religion. They both believe that they are being faithful to God as they walk out the demands of their religion. And yet, their path takes them in very different directions from one another.

CONSERVATIVE MENNONITES

It has been said that conservative Mennonites believe in the two "nuns": non-resistance and non-conformity. Non-resistance describes a conservative Mennonite's view of governmental authority and military force. Non-conformity describes a conservative Mennonite's view that a Christian community should be separate and distinct from the surrounding society.

Christian Aid Ministries (CAM) is a missionary organization that is supported by several networks of very conservative Mennonite and Amish churches. These traditional groups are usually divided from one another by various issues that might seem trivial to an outsider, and yet these groups all support CAM. CAM's statement of faith does a good job of accurately describing the beliefs that these divided conservative Mennonite and Amish churches hold in common.

Much of CAM's statement of faith is very similar to a statement of faith found in a typical evangelical religious organization. Conservative Mennonites hold a trinitarian view of God, believing in God the Father, Son, and Holy Spirit. They believe that the Bible is the divinely inspired Word of God. They believe there is one mediator between God and fallen man, the man Jesus Christ, who died and rose again to redeem mankind from his sin.

They believe that salvation is "by grace through faith in Christ, a free gift bestowed by God on all who believe in Christ, repent of their sins, are born again, and walk in newness of life."

Conservative Mennonites strongly believe in the sanctity of marriage. CAM puts it this way:

> We believe that marriage is designed by God to be the union of one man and one woman for life. Therefore, any sexual relationship outside this marriage is adultery. Furthermore, adultery, fornication, homosexuality, lesbianism, and any other sexual involvement is condemned by God.

CAM's statement of faith describes their view of non-resistance in this way:

> We believe that life is sacred and begins at conception and that Christians must not take part in any destruction of human life, born or unborn...We shall live a nonresistant lifestyle, without any acts of retaliation, demonstrating the love of Christ in our daily walk. Matt. 5:39-46; John 18:36; Rom. 12:19-21
>
> We believe that the church and state are ordained of God as separate entities in His divine plan, and that believers should honor rulers and be subject to their authority and pray for them. Rom. 13:1-7; I Peter 2:13-17

Conservative Mennonites believe that church and state are completely separate. Christians should pray for and honor those in governmental authority, but they should never participate in the military. Some of the most conservative Mennonites would believe that Christians should also not participate in government to any meaningful degree.

Conservative Mennonites would almost never become anti-war activists like those on the left. Conservative Mennonites would affirm that the government has the right and the responsibility to use the "sword" as described in Romans 13:4. Most conservative Mennonites would not have come out strongly against the Iraq War, for example. They simply believe that their community should not be involved in military service. Quite simply, many conservative Mennonites believe that the church should not be telling the government what to do but rather follow I Thessalonians 4:11: **"Make it your ambition to lead a quiet life: You should mind your own business and work with your hands, just as we told you."**

Some conservatives do become very involved in political issues. When they do become involved, it is usually on the conservative, right wing side of the political spectrum. Conservative talk-radio has had quite an influence on the political views of many in even the most conservative Mennonite communities.

Conservative Mennonites also believe in non-conformity. CAM's doctrinal statement reads:

We believe that the personal appearance and lifestyle of Christian men and women should be modest, free from worldly fashion and adornment, maintaining simplicity in all areas of life, living as strangers and pilgrims in this world, seeking a city not made with hands, eternal in the heavens.

Two scriptures that are used by conservative Mennonites to support their views on non-conformity are Romans 12:2, and James 4:4:

And do not be conformed to this world, but be transformed by the renewing of your mind, that you may prove what is that good and acceptable and perfect will of God (Romans 12:2)

Adulterers and adulteresses! Do you not know that friendship with the world is enmity with God? Whoever therefore wants to be a friend of the world makes himself an enemy of God. (James 4:4)

As part of their beliefs on non-conformity, many conservative Mennonite groups observe a strict dress code. The detail of this dress code varies from group to group. One group asks its members to wear black hats and suspenders. Another groups requires its members to wear plain suits. The women are required to wear head coverings, the appearance of which differs from group to group.

A favorite Scripture for those enforcing the dress code is I Peter 3:3-4: **"Do not let your adornment be merely outward—arranging the hair, wearing gold, or putting on fine apparel—rather let it be the hidden person of the heart, with the incorruptible beauty of a gentle and quiet spirit, which is very precious in the sight of God."**

The membership of the most conservative Mennonite groups is carefully guarded by gatekeepers who determine who is in and who is out. There is a list of rules which must be followed by those who are "in" the church. Some of these rules are written, some are unwritten. If a member strays too far from what is expected of him, he might find himself on the outside looking in.

Most of these groups believe in excommunication. When a member defies the authority and the rules of the group, he is excommunicated. This excommunication means that the person is no longer allowed to share Communion. It affects social interaction but in Mennonite groups does not usually include "shunning," an Amish practice in which the excommunicated member can have only a very limited and prescribed business or social interaction with members of the group.

CAM's statement declares: "We believe that the unrepentant, fallen brother or sister shall be excommunicated from the body of Christ in the spirit of love and shall be received back into fellowship upon repentance and amendment of life."

This is a very powerful form of social control. Some of these groups form closed communities, in which most of a member's friends, family, and business contacts are inside the group. If someone is excommunicated from such a group, he must start a completely new life. This is a daunting prospect for those who would consider leaving.

STAYING SEPARATE FROM THE WORLD

The authority figures in these groups assert their control over the group members. They try to ensure that nobody gets too close to the world. Group members are always reminded that they must be separate from the world.

Although it would seem that an evangelical Christian would believe many of the same things as a conservative Mennonite, Mennonites are reminded by their leaders what the differences are. Is the Baptist who lives down the street non-resistant? Does he believe that Christians should join the military? Is he non-conformist? Does he dress and act like the world?

With questions such as these, the lines are clearly drawn. Conservative Mennonites may be friendly with their Baptist neighbors, but they are also guarded. Christians from outside groups are worldly, and a good Mennonite needs to be somewhat careful in his interactions with them.

A conservative Mennonite lives out his life in a closed, Mennonite community. Community for a conservative includes people who dress like him, act like him, and believe like him.   He knows what is expected.

Obviously, the above description fully applies to only the most conservative groups today.   Sixty years ago, the above description would have applied to the majority of Mennonites in the United States. Mennonite churches today exist on a large spectrum, from the group described above to very liberal Mennonite churches.

LIBERAL MENNONITES

During the 1970's many Mennonites started moving away from the form of Christianity found in conservative Mennonite churches. Most liberal Mennonite churches can trace their roots back to conservative Mennonite churches like the ones described above. The founders of liberal Mennonite churches usually grew up in conservative Mennonite churches.   In some cases, they experienced suffocating control and religious legalism in those churches, which caused them to move in the opposite direction. They started Mennonite churches that are very different from the conservative Mennonite churches described above.

A liberal Mennonite church usually marches in lockstep with the political correctness and liberal social causes of our day.

A liberal Mennonite church is likely to place a large emphasis on "community". The community that they seek and celebrate is very different from the community found in a conservative Mennonite church. Community in the most conservative Mennonite churches is a closed community, complete with gatekeepers who work to keep the good Mennonites inside and the world outside. In contrast, a liberal Mennonite church has bulldozed the gates.   A liberal Mennonite church wants everyone to be included in their community.

Liberal Mennonite churches value multiculturalism.   They pride themselves in being open to various cultures and to people of different ethnic backgrounds.   They strive to build an ethnically diverse congregation.   They celebrate the members in their church who are minorities, such as African Americans, Latino-Americans, or Native

Americans. They spend an enormous amount of time and energy searching for hidden forms of racism and prejudice in society and in themselves.

Liberal Mennonite churches don't only embrace ethnic minorities in their community. They also embrace sexual minorities. For example, Community Mennonite Church of Lancaster writes the following in a statement of its values:

> Community Mennonite Church of Lancaster (CMCL) celebrates that we are a congregation with diversity of sexual orientation and gender identity. We publicly affirm that all persons, regardless of sexual orientation or gender identity, are equally eligible for membership, baptism, marriage, volunteer leadership, employment and pastoral ministry. We lament the history of the institutional church in condemning and excluding lesbian, gay, transgendered, bisexual and queer persons, and in condoning such discrimination by its silence. We commit ourselves to work diligently to end such oppression and discrimination.[8]

A liberal Mennonite church focuses on the love of God and the life of Jesus Christ. In their view, a loving God could not possibly condemn anyone to hell. They believe this in spite of the fact that Jesus taught about hell far more than anyone else in the Bible. If hell is not real, there is no need to be saved from hell. A liberal Mennonite church is unlikely to place much emphasis on personal sin or personal salvation.

There is one great exception to this view of sin. In the view of liberal Mennonites, perhaps the greatest personal sin that a man can commit is that of being prejudiced or intolerant. Liberal Mennonites closely examine their actions and reactions to see if there is anything slightly racist or intolerant in themselves. When they find something, they make a great show of repenting of these evils.

But generally speaking, sin is not really about the personal actions of individuals. Liberal Mennonite churches have gone out of their way

---

[8] www.communitymennonite.org/

to embrace and celebrate various forms of sexual "expression". It is difficult to teach the youth that they shouldn't engage in sexual intercourse with one another when the church embraces adults who are engaging in different forms of sexual immorality.

The moral universe of liberal Mennonites is divided into oppressors and the oppressed. The oppressors are those with power. They include large corporations, the United States government, and conservative, male-dominated American society in general. The oppressed include women, ethnic minorities, and sexual minorities. Sin has to do with the oppression and injustice that is committed by the oppressors against the oppressed.

There is therefore a great emphasis on oppression and injustice in liberal Mennonite churches. Community Mennonite Church writes its beliefs in this way: "We strive to RESPOND WITH JUSTICE, PEACEMAKING AND COMPASSION – We take seriously the church's call to address issues of social, economic and ecological justice and to challenge oppressive systems in our culture. We proclaim the building of shalom, peace and right relationships as the heart of the biblical message."

Most of all, liberal Mennonite churches emphasize peace. They believe that peacemaking involves opposing the oppressive forces in our society, such as the US military. Liberal Mennonites often become highly involved in left wing political activism on behalf of the ones they think are being oppressed. Some liberal Mennonites donned their pink pussyhats and marched on Washington in defiance of President Trump and his sexist and oppressive statements and policies. Many demonstrated against the wars in Iraq and Afghanistan. Thirty years ago, many liberal Mennonites united with the Sandinistas and other left wing groups against Ronald Reagan and his oppressive policies.

DEEP DIFFERENCES
Liberal and conservative Mennonites have deep differences, yet both groups believe that they are obeying Jesus. The conservative

Mennonite believes he is obeying the Lord as he prays that God would grant President Trump wisdom. The liberal Mennonite believes he is following Jesus as he joins a political demonstration that curses Trump in the most vulgar ways imaginable. The conservative Mennonite believes he is following Christ as he separates himself from the world; the liberal Mennonite feels just as convinced that he needs to embrace every marginalized group in this world.

It is not an exaggeration to say that these are two separate religions. They have a very different view of sin and salvation. They have very different views of God. Conservatives believe in the righteousness and holiness of God. They believe that He is the Judge, who will literally condemn men to hell. Liberals feel repelled by these views. They prefer to focus on the love of God and the times when God's servants challenged the power structures of their day in support of the oppressed. Both groups emphasize Scriptures that seem to support their views.

Both groups are very sincere. Some members of both groups might feel that they are "radical" Christians, living out Christianity the way that it is supposed to be lived out. The doctrine of both groups contains some biblical truth. And yet, why are these groups going in such different directions? How can the same Holy Spirit speak such different things? How can the scriptures speak such different things?

Sincerity alone does not bring one to God. Millions of Muslims are very sincere about their faith. Many pay a much higher price for their faith than the average Christian. Unfortunately, Islam cannot lead anyone into salvation. Islam cannot bring anyone into a living relationship with the living God. It is very easy to be sincerely deceived.

Is it really the Holy Spirit who leads churches to celebrate sexual perversion? Is it really the Holy Spirit that leads Christians to join with secular humanists in their crusade to force political correctness into every hidden corner of American society?

The Mennonite Middle

Probably most readers of this book are neither part of a very conservative Mennonite church like the ones I described above, nor are they part of a very liberal Mennonite Church. The majority of North American Mennonites are caught in the middle between the two extremes that I described. Many Mennonites are deeply concerned by the radical shift in doctrine that is taking place in their denomination. They are deeply concerned by the move away from biblical Christianity that is taking place in the Mennonite colleges. They are troubled by the way that gay marriage is gaining such overwhelming acceptance in the Mennonite colleges, and by the fact that the educated elite of the Mennonite church either supports what is taking place or is unwilling to confront it.

At the same time, those in the Mennonite middle are not willing to retreat back into closed religious communities that their grandparents grew up in. Mennonites in the middle are largely evangelical in their theology. They believe that the gospel needs to be preached, and that people must put their faith in Christ in order to be saved. They believe in heaven and hell. They may have been influenced to a degree by other forms of evangelical Christianity, including the Pentecostal and Charismatic movements. They desire to be faithful to the Scriptures and to be led by the Holy Spirit. They desire to reach their communities with the gospel of Jesus Christ. They are not willing to retreat into a closed religious community.

If you are somewhere in this Mennonite middle, this book is for you. In the following chapters, we will talk about how the Mennonite church ended up in its present condition. We will talk about the real enemy of the Mennonite church, the hijacker that has invaded the church and taken it down an evil path. We will talk about the calling that is upon the Mennonite church, and the path to reach that calling.

3 YODER AND THE CROSS

The changes taking place in the Mennonite church are powered by the changes taking place in the Mennonite educational institutions. In the Mennonite colleges and universities, conservative Mennonite students change their religion. They leave behind the faith of their fathers and become left-wing campus Christians. When they leave the campus, they form or join liberal Mennonite churches like the ones described in the previous chapter.

JOHN HOWARD YODER

One college professor who had a large impact upon the changes that took place in the Mennonite church was John Howard Yoder. Yoder was professor of theology at Goshen Biblical Seminary from 1965 to 1984, and served as its president from 1970 to 1973. In 1972, Yoder's book *The Politics of Jesus* was published. This book had an impact upon a generation of Mennonite students and scholars. Yoder and his book also received recognition and acclaim outside of Mennonite circles. In 2001 *Christianity Today* recognized this book as one of the most important Christian books of the 20th century.

In *The Politics of Jesus* Yoder emphasizes the centrality of the cross of Christ. His definition of the cross is quite different from the conservative evangelical definition. Yoder defines the cross of Christ as the "the political, legally to be expected result of a moral clash with the powers ruling his society"(Yoder, p. 129).[9]

---

[9] This and following quotations of Yoder's work come from Yoder's 2nd edition of *The Politics of Jesus* (1994.

According to Yoder, the powers ruling society included religious systems, political systems, traditions, and other means by which human societies are ruled. These powers are necessary for human society to function, but they are also fallen. The way these powers work and control the societies of men is not the way that Christ's kingdom works. These powers can't just be removed, because they perform a necessary function. Instead, their sovereignty needs to be broken. Yoder writes:

> **If then God is going to save his creatures in their humanity, the powers cannot simply be destroyed or set aside or ignored. Their sovereignty must be broken. This is what Jesus did, concretely and historically, by living a genuinely free and human existence. This life brought him, as any genuinely human existence will bring anyone, to the cross. In his death the powers, in this case the most worthy, weighty representatives of Jewish Religion and Roman politics acted in collusion. Like everyone, he too was subject, but in his case quite willingly, to these powers. He accepted his own status of submission (Yoder, p. 144).**

Jesus clashed with these powers when He refused to do things their way. The powers ruling human society use violence and dominion to get things done. Jesus refused to work this way. Although Jesus was repeatedly tempted to use violent methods to bring forth his kingdom, He refused that temptation.. He refused to use violence to do the things that needed to be done. He refused to use violence to bring forth His kingdom on the earth. Therefore the "powers", the representatives of Jewish Religion and Roman politics, condemned Jesus to death. By refusing to compromise and do things the world's way, Jesus was victorious over the powers as He went to the cross.

In one sense Jesus was subject to the powers because He accepted their sentence of death upon himself. But by refusing to operate according to their rules, to their ways of violence, He defeated them. By refusing to operate according to their ways, He delegitimized their ways of doing things and showed that men don't need to live that way.

Yoder believed that there need to be communities of believers that walk the same way Jesus walked. Instead of trying to dominate one another and use one another the way the powers that rule society do, they love and serve one another. They refuse to recognize or allow into their community the divisions caused by racism and nationalism. They refuse to use violence or other forms of power to get their way. These communities are so different from the communities of this world, that these communities will be persecuted by the surrounding communities. Yoder writes: "The believer's cross is, like that of Jesus, the price of social nonconformity." (Yoder, p. 96)

Yoder writes, "The cross of Jesus was a political punishment; and when Christians are made to suffer by government, it is usually because of the practical import of their faith and the doubt they cast upon the rulers' claim to be Benefactor" (Yoder, p.125). In other words, the community of believers should refuse to pretend that the political rulers of its society are benefactors, good leaders who work for the good of all. The community of believers should refuse to support and participate in the violent causes and crusades of its government. As the church refuses to support the government's wrong use of power, it will be persecuted. This persecution is the cross of Christ that the church must carry.

Therefore, in Yoder's view, the cross that Christians must carry is closely connected to pacifism. As Christians refuse to participate in government-sponsored violence such as war and the death penalty, they take up their cross and follow Jesus, humbly accepting whatever punishment the government dishes out for their stand.

FOUNDATIONAL DOCTRINES

As Yoder redefined the cross, he seemed to question many foundational doctrines. Yoder believed that many Scriptures that seemed to support conservative evangelical doctrines were actually speaking about something completely different. For example, Galatians 2:16 says that a man **"is not justified by the works of the law but by faith in Jesus Christ…for by the works of the law no flesh shall be justified."** Yoder points out that Galatians 2 is part of a discussion on whether Jewish and Gentile Christians were to be part of the same fellowship. In other words, being justified by grace through faith is not about the salvation of an individual. It is about joining together into one, two groups of people who used to be divided. This understanding of justification is quite different from what an evangelical usually means by justification.

Yoder claims that Paul saw sin very differently from how evangelical Christians see it. He thinks that Paul did not experience deep anguish because he was a sinner and separated from God. He says that Paul's sin was the fact that he tried to keep the Gentiles from joining the household of God. When things were set right in his life, he did not start trusting in God's righteousness instead of his own. When things were set right in his life, he reached out to the Gentiles to bring them into the kingdom. In other words, sin has more to do with the divisions between people groups than it does the dark and evil motives hidden in the heart of man.

Likewise, Yoder doesn't believe that the Law of Moses was given primarily to expose the sin of mankind and thus show the need for a Savior. He disagrees with Martin Luther's translation that the Law is a schoolmaster that teaches us that we are sinners who need a savior. He prefers the interpretation that the Law was a "custodian" that gave order to people's lives as they waited for the Messiah.

Yoder also didn't like the conservative evangelical focus on the transformation of men's hearts. He writes, "Conservative evangelicalism focuses its call for change upon the will of the individual because it believes that when the individual heart is turned in another direction the rest is sure to follow." Yoder believes that this approach is wrong. He thinks that when one focuses on one central point such as the transformation of people's hearts, believing that will determine the wellbeing of people, one automatically ends up sacrificing other things for the greater good. A person with such a belief ends up sacrificing the "life and welfare of one's self, one's neighbor, and (of course) the enemy" because he is so focused on changing hearts. Yoder disagrees with those who say a Christian should first try to change the hearts of individuals through faith in Christ in hopes that their transformed lives will then change society. Yoder calls this view part of "nonbiblical thought patterns" (p. 221).

In general, Yoder didn't seem to like the evangelical emphasis on sin, salvation, and the transformation of individual hearts and lives. Of more importance to Yoder than the fact that an individual has sin removed and comes into right standing before God was that the barriers between people were removed as they came into fellowship with one another and with God. Yoder has very little to say about the need for personal repentance of one's sins and the receiving of Jesus Christ into one's life.

THE IDOLS OF PEACE AND PACIFISM

In Christianity, there is a cross that men are called to carry, and the cross that Christ himself carried. The cross of Christ is at the very center of Christianity. Evangelical Christians believe that Jesus is "the Lamb of God, who takes away the sin of the world" (John 1:29). Jesus is the perfect sacrifice, the Savior of mankind, the one who paid the price for our sin as He died on the cross. He is the one who defeated sin and death as he rose from the dead. Through His sacrifice, men can come into relationship with the living God. Through faith in the name of Jesus, people can be saved from their sin and receive eternal life. This is the good news, the Gospel of Jesus Christ.

Yoder de-emphasized these foundational biblical truths. Instead of focusing on what Christ did for us at the cross, he focused on the one of the side effects of the cross – the reconciliation that takes place between men. Instead of focusing on the reconciliation that takes place between God and man at the cross, he constantly emphasized the reconciliation that takes place between people through Christ.

When Yoder speaks of the gospel, he does not emphasize the fact that Jesus died for our sins and that we can be reconciled to the living God through covenant. Yoder emphasizes a gospel that proclaims the removal of barriers between ethnic groups, love for one's enemies and the renunciation of violence. Yoder writes, "It is the Good News that my enemy and I are united, through no merit or work of our own, in a new humanity that forbids henceforth my ever taking his or her life in my hands" (Yoder, p. 221).

Yoder never went so far as to actually deny the truth of foundational Christian doctrines. He always claimed that he was just emphasizing truths that had been ignored by evangelical Christians, without actually denying the doctrines of evangelical Christianity. Nevertheless, Yoder and other Mennonite professors shifted the spiritual focus of the Mennonite colleges. The focus shifted away from Jesus Christ, crucified and risen again. The focus shifted away from reconciliation between God and man through the cross of Jesus Christ. The focus shifted towards peace and pacifism, the reconciliation between men.

When the work of Christ loses its central place in Christianity, it opens the door for something else to take its place. The reconciliation between men became so important to Yoder and other Anabaptists, that it began to take the place of Jesus Christ, crucified and risen again. The idols of peace and pacifism began to take their place at the center of the Mennonite religious institutions.

As Mennonite scholars stopped emphasizing individual salvation in favor of peace and pacifism, the generation of Mennonite students passing through the colleges were influenced by the change of emphasis. Many of these students never actually experienced true conversion and the forgiveness of their sins. Many never had a genuine encounter with God. They never heard his voice or felt his overwhelming presence. Christianity for them is just the moral example of a man who lived a long time ago. Consequently, Christianity becomes just an ethical system that is applied to world social problems such as war and poverty.

Christianity is 100 percent supernatural. It is impossible to live out the commands of Christ unless the supernatural love of God is flowing through you. It is impossible to actually love your enemy, unless you have had a transforming encounter with the living God, and He has put the very love of Jesus inside your heart. When Christians stop emphasizing personal conversion and the transforming power of the Holy Spirit, they lose everything.

WHAT IS THE SWORD?

As Mennonite scholars redefined the cross to make it almost indistinguishable from their belief in pacifism, they also redefined the legitimate role of government. Yoder believed that military force was not within a government's legitimate authority.

Paul declares in Romans 13 that the sword is given to the rulers of this earth, and that they do not bear that sword in vain:

> **For rulers are not a terror to good works, but to evil. Do you want to be unafraid of the authority? Do what is good, and you will have praise from the same. For he is God's minister to you for good. But if you do evil, be afraid; for he does not bear the sword in vain; for he is God's minister, an avenger to execute wrath on him who practices evil (Romans 13:3-4).**

Rulers are to use the sword to execute God's anger upon the one who practices evil.

Yoder claimed that the sword (*machaira*) given by God to civil authority in Romans 13 was just a long dagger, not a real sword. It was a symbol of police authority and judicial authority, not military authority. Therefore, Yoder believed that the church should never support the government in waging war or in capital punishment. When the government persecutes the church for taking this stand, that persecution was the cross of Christ that the church should carry.

In Romans 13, the word we translate as sword is *machaira*. This is the same word that is used in almost every New Testament passage that speaks of swords, and in most of those passages it is clear that *machaira* is a weapon of death and war. *Machaira* is a generic New testament term for sword. Quite simply, the sword of Romans 13 is a military weapon. If that passage were written using modern language, it could legitimately be written: "If you do evil, be afraid, because the governmental rulers are not given the assault rifle in vain."

Yoder didn't only say that Christians should not be involved in the military; he went a step further and declared that the military force of the government was itself illegitimate. Not only were Christians not to participate, they should speak out and condemn the government's use of military power.

MENNONITES IN WARTIME

Yoder wrote this book as the Vietnam War was winding down. He wrote this book during a period of almost unprecedented activism and anger targeted against the United States government and its war in Vietnam. In this environment, Yoder's book connected with a generation of young, idealistic Mennonites who resisted America's military adventures.

During previous wars, Mennonites were often rejected and ostracized by their surrounding communities. For example, Mennonites suffered for the sake of their faith in World War I.

On April 6, 1917, America declared war on Germany and entered World War I. As the nation mobilized for war, an unprecedented level of pro-war propaganda was unleashed by the US government and other sources. The government established The Committee on Public Information (CPI) to lead its propaganda effort. Millions of pro-war posters were produced that demonized the German enemy. The film industry produced pro-war movies such as "The Kaiser, Beast of Berlin" and played them in packed movie theaters. The music industry produced a steady stream of pro-war, patriotic songs.

This propaganda effort was not only used to drum up support for the war. It was also used to malign those groups who were not supportive of the war effort. Some of the propaganda targeted German Americans, socialists, and pacifists as slackers and draft dodgers.

Needless to say, German-speaking, nonresistant Mennonites were not the most popular people during that time. In Kansas, Mennonites faced mob violence. Some Mennonites were tarred and feathered as they resisted the nationwide call to arms. Some were imprisoned for their refusal to fight.

In World War II, America was attacked on its own soil, and the nation became very unified in its support for the war effort. The Selective Training and Service Act of 1940 made it possible for nonresistant

Mennonites to avoid combat by serving in alternative service or noncombatant military positions. Therefore, Mennonites faced less outright persecution from the US government in World War II.

Nevertheless, Mennonites in World War II faced the criticism and ostracism of the surrounding society because of their beliefs and their refusal to "do their part". In rural communities, Mennonite farmers prospered as the price for agricultural products increased during the war years. Meanwhile, the farms of their non-Mennonite neighbors suffered as the young men went off to war. This led to a lot of resentment in farming communities against the Mennonites.

In general, the Mennonites lived at the fringes of American society. They were often not considered to be completely American. Many of them spoke German, in a century when Germans were often the enemy. They looked different, dressed differently, and lived in separate communities.

But during the Vietnam War, things changed. For one of the few times in American history, a large portion of American society turned against its own government, and against the war effort in Vietnam. During the Vietnam War, the counterculture became popular, as hippies and socialists formed their own movements and communities. During the Vietnam War, pacifism became popular on college campuses and in the counterculture.

This created a great opportunity for Mennonite students. Instead of being a rejected, despised community, Mennonite students could connect to the larger counterculture. Mennonites were already a counterculture, never fully integrated into American society. Mennonites were pacifists who refused to participate in America's military endeavors. For the first time, in their American history, Mennonites had the opportunity to join the cutting edge of a social movement.

This transformation could only take place in a college setting. Mennonites in those days lived in closed, religious communities. The social control found in those communities kept most people from straying too far from the beaten path.

But on the Mennonite college campuses the climate was open to change. Always when a Mennonite student leaves his rural home community for college, it is possible for radical change to take place. He leaves behind the world that he knew. He leaves behind family and friends. He is leaves behind his connection to local church life. He enters a new world. Change is especially likely when the college campus subjects this person to new ideas and testing circumstances.

WHAT DOES IT MEAN TO FOLLOW CHRIST?

The Mennonite college student who attended one of the Mennonite colleges in the 1970's typically entered college as a committed Christian. During his time in college, he changed his ideas about what it meant to be a committed Christian. In the Mennonite community that he came from, being a committed Christian meant being separate from the world. It meant not drinking, not smoking, and not engaging in sexual immorality. It meant dressing differently from the world, going to church, and following the rules that were laid down by the church.

Now in college, that student learned a different definition of radical Christianity. Under the influence of John Howard Yoder and other professors, the student learned that following Jesus meant a conflict between Christians and a corrupt and violent political system. Under the influence of Yoder and other professors, the student learned about corporate sin, the sin of the American system. Radical Christianity had more to do with opposing the war in Vietnam than it did with preaching the gospel to unbelievers.

In college, the Mennonite student learned that the cross of Jesus was "the legally expected outcome of a moral and political clash with the powers ruling society." Radical Christians were not those who preached the evangelical gospel of salvation and transformation. Radical Christians clashed with the power that ruled society. Radical Christians confronted the sins of America.

In the colleges, Mennonite students learned to look at the world in a new way. They learned to despise American influence and military power. And they learned to despise America's "Christian" heritage.

The Mennonite colleges taught the students about the failures of American evangelical Christianity. They learned that Christians were complicit in many of the nation's greatest sins. In college they studied slavery, and the way that the white, Protestant social order created and supported the institution of slavery in America. They studied the sins of America's founding fathers, many of whom were slaveholders. They studied America's genocidal campaigns against Native Americans, campaigns that at times received moral support from the church. They studied the internment of the Japanese Americans in concentration camps during World War II. They studied the ways in which the American church supported the American government as it committed these atrocities.

In short, they learned to despise American evangelical Christians whom they saw as being complicit in America's sins. Evangelical Christians were the collaborators, who supported the evil American military establishment. Evangelical Christians were the patriotic supporters of America's wars of aggression. Accordingly, evangelical Christians could not be genuine Christians. Genuine Christians were those who took up their cross and followed Jesus by embracing pacifism and opposing America's military adventures.

OPPRESSORS AND THE OPPRESSED

The Christianity that became acceptable on Mennonite college campuses was a Christianity that took up the cause of the oppressed against the oppressors, a Christianity that married Christian faith with the causes favored by the campus left.

This left-wing campus Christianity separates the world into oppressors and oppressed. The oppressors are the sinners, and the oppressed are the victims. White males are the ultimate oppressors. Heterosexual men and women who are not sympathetic to the plight of gays and lesbians are oppressors. Republicans are oppressors. Evangelical Christians are usually classed as oppressors, because they vote for oppressive, conservative politicians and refuse to celebrate homosexuality.

African Americans are victims. Native Americans are victims. Hispanics are victims. Illegal immigrants are victims. Women are victims. Gays and lesbians are victims. Members of the Democratic Party are victims, and the supporters of victims.

Those who fall in the "oppressor' category are guilty of all the evil found in this world. This collective guilt operates in a way similar to the "original sin" of traditional Christianity. However, the sin of oppression is not washed away by the blood of Jesus. The only way one can be purged of the sin of oppression is to take the side of the victims in the war against the oppressors, or better yet, become a victim yourself. Only then can you truly be innocent.

Because individual sin does not really exist in this system of thought, it is impossible for victims to really be sinners. It is actually taught in our nation's universities that blacks cannot be racist because racism equals prejudice plus power. Only white Christian males hold power; therefore, only white Christian males can truly be racist.

To know who is right and who is wrong in any conflict, you simply need to examine which group the combatants come from. For example, when the "Black Lives Matter" rioters clash with the police, their lawless violence is not taken into account. The only thing that really matters is the fact that they are black or are supporting a "black" cause. Therefore, they are part of the oppressed, no matter how many people they beat up. The police, on the other hand, are obviously the oppressors.

Members of the Christian left instinctively side with groups such as "Black Lives Matter". They do not need to look into the details of the case to see who was actually oppressing whom. They already know the answer by looking at the groups the combatants come from. Blacks are members of the oppressed groups. White cops are oppressors. The details of the conflict do not really matter.

Life experience and common sense informs the average person that human evil simply does not work this way. Anyone who knows women knows that women have the same propensity for evil as men. Anyone who has lived among people of different ethnic groups knows that racism is not only found in white people. We are all part of one race, the human race, and that race is fallen. Every individual, of every race and gender, is capable of great evil.

On the campus, left wing Christians learn about peacemaking and social justice. This inevitably means taking the side of one of the "oppressed" groups against members of the oppressor groups. Mennonite college students study the oppressive power structures found in American society and the ways in which those power structures oppress the members of the oppressed groups and work for the benefit of the oppressive groups.

SOCIAL JUSTICE?

"Social justice" isn't quite the same as real justice. Social justice movements such as "Black Lives Matter" fight for the rights of various oppressed groups. Inevitably, such movements end up making many judgments based on the group that people belong to, instead of looking at the actual facts of a situation. In contrast, true justice is blind. The statues of Lady Justice that represent our justice system are of a woman who is blindfolded, holding a set of scales. When a person appears before court, the justice system is supposed to be blind to the race of the accused, blind to his wealth and social position. The only thing that matters are the facts of the case.

Martin Luther King, Jr., spoke to the same point in his famous "I have a dream" speech when he said, "I have a dream that my four little children will one day live in a nation where they will not be judged by the color of their skin, but by the content of their character." [10]

---

[10] "Martin Luther King Jr. - Acceptance Speech". Nobelprize.org. Nobel Media AB 2014. Web. 4 Jul 2017.
<http://www.nobelprize.org/nobel_prizes/peace/laureates/1964/king-acceptance.html>

For example, the Black Lives Matter movement holds demonstrations that protest the shooting of black men by police officers. The social justice warrior will look at the number of black men who have been shot by police officers, and immediately conclude that a great injustice has taken place. He will think that he is fighting for justice as he demonstrates in the streets.

In fact, if you want to know whether or not an injustice has occurred, it is necessary to look at each case in detail. This can only be done in a courtroom. A mob demonstrating on the streets jumps to conclusions based on partial information, particularly the race of the police officer and the victim. This mob is unable to make fair judgment that will bring justice to the situation.

Sometimes when the facts are presented, it turns out that the police officer had legitimate reasons to fear for his life when he took the shot. The policeman reacted the way he was trained to react, and, in fact, no injustice took place. In other cases, a police officer jumped to unjustified conclusions and gunned down an innocent man. In such cases, that police officer needs to be prosecuted to the full extent of the law. The point is, you cannot determine if an injustice took place simply by looking at the race of the shooters and the victims. Such an approach will inevitably lead to wrong conclusions. Such an approach will inevitably lead to injustice.

In the name of social justice, the left judges many things according to the category in which they place someone. They judge according to the color of one's skin and according to other categories that help them determine the oppressed from the oppressors. They call this social justice, but it inevitably leads to injustice.

In fact, left wing campus Christians have some things in common with Communists and other radical Marxists. Communists judged everyone according to their class. According to Communist ideology, the oppressors were the capitalists, the bourgeoisie who owned the means of production. The oppressed class was the workers, the proletariat.

The Communists judged men based upon their social class. They did not need to know anything about a man's private life to determine whether or not he deserved to be sent to the gulag. It didn't matter if a man spent his life helping his neighbors and serving the poor. The only thing that mattered was the class that he belonged to. The capitalists were evil. The workers were good. That was all anyone really needed to know.

The Communists brought their brand of social justice as they overturned the social system, shipping the capitalists off to the gulag to pay for their crimes and setting up a system that supposedly helped the workers. In reality, almost everyone suffered under Communism, especially the peasants. Mass murder and starvation took place with depressing regularity in nearly every Communist nation.

Nevertheless, the left-wing campus Christians often made common cause with the Communists. They supported the Sandinistas in Nicaragua. They demonstrated with other leftists against the US military buildup. They absolutely despised Ronald Reagan, who believed that Communism could and should actually be defeated.

The truth is, left wing campus Christians are really only comfortable when they are attacking American, conservative Christians. When the atrocities of other groups are exposed, they always try to change the subject back to their preferred punching bag. When Communist atrocities were exposed in different countries, the left wing campus Christians try to change the subject to the atrocities committed by dictators supported by America.

Today, there is actual genocide taking place in Syria and Iraq at the hands of the ISIS Islamic extremists. Left wing campus Christians do not really feel comfortable talking about the murder and mayhem committed by Islamic terrorists. In their world view, Muslims belong in the "oppressed" category, while most Christians belong in the "oppressor" category. Therefore, it is very difficult for them to look at the atrocities committed by the "oppressed" Muslims. They would much rather focus on the Islamophobia of the oppressive American Christian than on the mass murders committed by the jihadis.

And so, if you talk of the thousands of Christians that are being beheaded and tortured by ISIS, the left wing campus Christian will try to change the topic. He will say, "What about the Crusades? During the Crusades, Christians invaded the Middle East and killed thousands of people. Christians are just as bad as ISIS! "

In this way, a left-wing campus Christian tries to change the topic back to the sins of the oppressors against the oppressed, no matter how difficult that task might seem. He tries to ignore the genocide that is taking place right under his nose by changing the topic to something bad that Christians did, even if he has to go back 1000 years in history to find that bad thing.

In many cases, this attempt to change the topic becomes ridiculous. Yes, 1000 years ago, some medieval Christians responded to 500 years of Islamic jihad by fighting a ruthless "holy war" of their own. How in the world does that justify the genocide that is taking place today? America has never supported a crusade against Islam. The war in Iraq might have been ill advised, but it was certainly not a religious crusade! George Bush used every opportunity to tell everybody what a wonderful, peaceful religion Islam is.

Left-wing campus Christians hate any conversation that shines a negative light upon one of their "oppressed" groups. They will never hold demonstrations against the atrocities committed by ISIS, because ISIS is not on their list of oppressors. They will usually try to change the topic back to their preferred target – conservative American Christians, or perhaps the modern state of Israel.

WHAT DOES IT REALLY MEAN TO "TAKE UP YOUR CROSS"?
During the 1970's thousands of conservative Mennonites became left wing campus Christians in the Mennonite colleges and universities. When these students left the campus, some left the Christian faith entirely, but many stayed connected to the Mennonite church. They became the educated elite that dominate the religious institutions and structures of the Mennonite church today.

Yoder defined the cross as "the legally expected outcome of a moral and political clash with the powers ruling society." This definition influenced a generation of liberal Mennonites. Even today, liberal

Mennonites are likely to believe that the cross they are supposed to carry involves social and political activism against the powers that rule society for the sake of oppressed groups against their oppressors.

Does the cross really have very much to do with the Mennonite belief in peace and nonresistance? Is the cross really the "price of social non-conformity" as Yoder taught, or the price of not supporting the violence of the state? Is this view of the cross biblical?

First of all, it is important to distinguish between the price that Jesus paid on the cross and the price that all believers pay when they take up their cross and follow Jesus. Jesus paid a price that no man can pay. Jesus is "the Lamb that was slain, who takes away the sin of the world." He was the perfect sacrifice, the one who paid the price of our sins.

This sacrifice is always supreme. No matter what price the followers of Jesus may pay, they cannot save themselves; and they cannot pay the price of sin for themselves. This must always be remembered. When Christians forget this distinction, then Jesus becomes just a moral example for mankind, instead of the Savior of the world.

But, of course, the Bible also speaks of the cross that believers must carry. Jesus said to his disciples, **"If anyone desires to come after Me, let him deny himself, and take up his cross, and follow Me. For whoever desires to save his life will lose it, but whoever loses his life for My sake will find it"** (Matthew 16:24-25).

So what is the cross that believers carry? It is useful to look at the cross that the disciples and apostles of Christ bore. If we look at their example, particularly in the book of Acts, we can learn much about the cross that the followers of Jesus should carry.

The Roman Empire was one of the most cruel and monstrous empires in history. Did the apostles carry their cross and pay a price because they refused to participate in Roman military power? Did they pay a price because they refused to support the death penalty? Did they pay a price because they refused to involve themselves in the Roman military system? In fact, the apostles had little to say about these things. They didn't actually say whether or not it was permissible for

Christians to join the Roman army or take positions in the Roman governmental system.

The apostles paid a very high price for their faith. The price they paid had much more to do with their testimony of Jesus Christ than with anything else. The apostles testified of Jesus Christ, crucified and risen again. They confirmed this testimony with great miracles. This testimony shook the world, and this testimony caused the Jews and the Romans to persecute the church.

In Acts 3 we read about this testimony. We read about Peter and John going to pray in the temple, when they meet the lame man who asks for alms. Peter says to the lame man: **"Silver and gold I do not have, but what I do have I give you: In the name of Jesus Christ of Nazareth, rise up and walk."** The lame man began walking, leaping, and praising God. Peter and John went with the lame man into the temple where Peter testified of Christ. He preached:

> **"Men of Israel, why do you marvel at this? Or why look so intently at us, as though by our own power or godliness we had made this man walk? The God of Abraham, Isaac, and Jacob, the God of our fathers, glorified His Servant Jesus, whom you delivered up and denied in the presence of Pilate, when he was determined to let Him go. But you denied the Holy One and the Just, and asked for a murderer to be granted to you, and killed the Prince of life, whom God raised from the dead, of which we are witnesses. And His name, through faith in His name, has made this man strong, whom you see and know. Yes, the faith which comes through Him has given him this perfect soundness in the presence of you all....Repent therefore and be converted, that your sins may be blotted out, so that times of refreshing may come from the presence of the Lord, and that He may send Jesus Christ, who was preached to you before, whom heaven must receive until the times of restoration of all things, which God has spoken by the mouth of all His holy prophets since the world began"(Acts 3:12-21).**

The religious leaders were greatly disturbed by this testimony because Peter and John "taught the people and preached in Jesus the resurrection from the dead." They put Peter and John in custody for the night. The next day Peter and John were brought before the religious leaders and rulers. Again, Peter testified with power:

> **"Let it be known to you all, and to all the people of Israel, that by the name of Jesus Christ of Nazareth, whom you crucified, whom God raised from the dead, by Him this man stands here before you whole. This is the 'stone which was rejected by you builders, which has become the chief cornerstone.' Nor is there salvation in any other, for there is no other name under heaven given among men by which we must be saved"(Acts 4:10-12).**

The religious leaders and rulers discussed how they might stop this gospel from spreading. They decided to severely threaten Peter and the others to stop testifying in the name of Jesus. When they threatened Peter, he responded, **"Whether it is right in the sight of God to listen to you more than to God, you judge. For we cannot but speak the things which we have seen and heard."**

After threatening Peter and John a second time, they released them. Peter and John joined with the believers to cry out to God for greater boldness, and more miracles, so that they could continue to testify of Christ with power. They prayed,

> **"Now, Lord, look on their threats, and grant to Your servants that with all boldness they may speak Your word, by stretching out Your hand to heal, and that signs and wonders may be done through the name of Your Holy Servant Jesus."**

> **After praying, the place where they were staying was shaken. And they were all filled with the Holy Spirit and they spoke the Word of God with boldness** (Acts 4:28-31).

What is the cross that the apostles carried? The apostles preached the gospel wherever they went. Sometimes they preached for people to repent and be baptized. Sometimes they preached about the Law and the prophets. Sometimes they preached about creation. They always preached Jesus Christ. It was the testimony of Jesus Christ, crucified and risen from the dead, that caused the disciples to be persecuted.

This persecution that resulted from the testimony of Jesus Christ was the cross that the apostles carried.

It is impossible to separate the cross that Christians are to carry from the testimony of Jesus Christ. Everywhere Paul went, he testified of Christ. Everywhere he went, he faced persecution because of that testimony. He did not spend his time preaching about the evils of the Roman empire. He called on his listeners to repent and believe in Jesus. He backed up his testimony with supernatural power.

It is the same today. If you testify of Jesus Christ today in America, you will face resistance and even persecution. If you preach the gospel to Muslims, you may well face the very same type of persecution that Peter faced.

I am involved in starting schools in different nations that train Christians to testify to Muslims. Every student who passes through those schools knows what it means to testify and what it means to pay a price for their testimony. Nobody graduates from our schools without being able to preach the gospel of Jesus Christ in Islamic communities.

We make things much too complicated. Who really cares about your politics? Who really cares about the details of your beliefs on various political and social issues? What is important is Jesus. If you testify of Jesus, you will pay a price, and you will carry your cross.

THE OVERCOMERS

When someone walks the way of the cross and obeys God unto death, incredible, world-changing power is unleashed. All through history, when someone hears the voice of God and obeys unto death, the powers of the heavenly realm are shaken. This leads to the overthrow of kingdoms and nations. This leads to the disintegration of empires.

This is seen in the ultimate victory over the devil and his angels. In Revelation 12, John describes a war taking place in the heavenly realms. This is a war between the devil and his angels and Michael and his angels. This war is connected to the saints who are on the earth. The final victory of this heavenly war is described in Revelation 12.

And war broke out in heaven: Michael and his angels fought with the dragon; and the dragon and his angels fought, but they did not prevail, nor was a place found for them in heaven any longer. So the great dragon was cast out, that serpent of old, called the Devil and Satan, who deceives the whole world; he was cast to the earth, and his angels were cast out with him.

Then I heard a loud voice saying in heaven, "Now salvation, and strength, and the kingdom of our God, and the power of His Christ have come, for the accuser of our brethren, who accused them before our God day and night, has been cast down."

And they overcame him by the blood of the Lamb and by the word of their testimony, and they did not love their lives to the death (Revelation 12:7-11).

The Bible says that there was not a place found in heaven for the devil and his angels any longer. Michael and his angels cast out the devil and his angels down to the earth, where they rage upon the earth for a short time, knowing that the time for them to be cast into the pit is very, very near.

This great victory is connected to the saints. When speaking of this great victory, John says, "They overcame by the blood of the lamb, by the word of their testimony, and they loved not their lives to the death." Even though the battle was fought in the heavenly realm between the angels of Michael and Satan, the victory was won because the saints overcame on the earth. These saints overcame "by the blood of the Lamb, by the word of their testimony, and they loved not their lives unto death. "

These saints overcame by the blood of the Lamb. The blood of the Lamb represents the cross of Christ. Because of the blood of the Lamb, the saints have a blood covenant with the living God. They belong to God, and He belongs to them.

This covenant is not one-sided. The Lord gave everything He had for the saints at the cross. The saints also take up their cross and follow Jesus. They do this by the word of their testimony and not loving their lives to the death. The saints overcome not only by the blood of the Lamb but also by the word of their testimony. They speak the Word of God, fearlessly and powerfully. And when it comes time for them to pay a price for their testimony, they give their lives. They love not their life unto the death.

This is the cross. The blood of the Lamb is the cross that Jesus carried. The testimony of the Lamb unto death is the cross that the disciples of Jesus carry. This cross is carried by those who love God more than their own life, those who speak His word fearlessly. This is the cross that the apostles carried. The apostles did not have much to say about the death penalty or Roman military power. They preached Jesus Christ and him crucified. They demonstrated the power of the risen Christ.

They overcame by the blood of the Lamb, by the word of their testimony, and they loved not their lives to the death. Everywhere they went, they spoke the Word of God. They confronted kings and rulers and religious leaders. They were unafraid to preach the gospel. They didn't merely live in their closed communities; they went where God sent them. And when it came time for them to die because of their testimony, they willingly gave their lives.

THE PATH OF THE CROSS
A fuller definition of the cross can be found in Philippians 2:5-11. In this Scripture we read about the path of the cross that Jesus walked, and we can learn about the path that we are called to walk:

> Let this mind be in you which was also in Christ Jesus, who, being in the form of God, did not consider it robbery to be equal with God, but made Himself of no reputation, taking the form of a bondservant, and coming in the likeness of men. And being found in appearance as a man, He humbled Himself and became obedient to the point of death, even the death of the cross.

Therefore God also has highly exalted Him and given Him the name which is above every name, that at the name of Jesus every knee should bow, of those in heaven, and of those on earth, and of those under the earth, and that every tongue should confess that Jesus Christ is Lord, to the glory of God the Father.

In this Scripture we see extreme humility, servanthood, and obedience unto death, all because of love. This is the path of the cross. Jesus was in very nature God, and yet he didn't hold on to his godhood. He humbled himself and became of no reputation. He took on human flesh and walked the earth as a man. He came not only as a man, but as a bondservant, essentially a slave. Even this was not the end of Christ's humility. He humbled himself yet further, until he hung naked on the cross and suffered the most humiliating and painful death that evil men could devise. He did this because of love.

Likewise, those who take up their cross and follow Jesus will be willing to humble themselves as Jesus did, as the apostles did. Paul said of the apostles: **"Being reviled, we bless; being persecuted, we endure; being defamed, we entreat. We have been made as the filth of the world, the offscouring of all things until now"** (I Corinthians 4:12-13).

Those who carry their cross will not exalt themselves. They will humble themselves and seek the glory of the Son of God instead of their own glory. They will not think themselves too great for any task that God gives them. They will pour out their lives and serve the ones that He asks them to serve.

The cross is complete obedience to the point of death, because of love. Jesus not only humbled himself. He became obedient to the point of death. He obeyed the Father every day of his life. He cemented his will to the will of the Father, declaring **"the Son only does what he sees the Father doing."**

This complete obedience led to the cross. At the cross Jesus struggled with the task that was before him. Once again, He chose the will of the Father, saying "Not my will, but thy will be done."

Those who take up their cross learn to obey the voice of the Lord. They become the sons of the living God who hear the voice of the Father every day and choose to obey Him. As they walk with the Father and obey him daily, they experience much joy and blessing. However, if they follow the path to the end, it will cost them everything.

This obedience unto death is most clearly seen in the area of testimony. The apostles refused to stay silent. They obeyed the leading of the Holy Spirit as they opened their mouths and testified of Jesus Christ with great power. Even when their lives were threatened, they continued to obey and testify. In the end, they gave their lives because of their testimony.

Great humility and even obedience unto death mean nothing unless they are being done because of love. Most of all, the path of the cross is a path of supernatural love. **God so loved the world that He gave his only begotten son** (John 3:16). The cross is the ultimate demonstration of God's love. It is where God showed just how much He loved us. Those who walk the path of the cross will grow in love. Everything they do will be done because of love. God will flow through them like a river, as God uses them to pour out His love upon the earth. There will be no cost too high, no task too difficult, because of the love that is inside them.

The path of the cross is a wonderful road, a road of great adventure. It is a path of supernatural power, supernatural love, and great joy. It is a love of world-shaking testimony. However, if you walk that road to its conclusion, it will cost you everything, even your lif

4 PEACE AND PALESTINE

VERBRANDE BRUG

I live in the small village known as Verbrande Brug (Burned Bridge) on the outskirts of Brussels, Belgium. Several years ago I sat down with my neighbors at a community gathering that was organized to connect the neighborhood. I found myself sitting at a table with the farmer who lives down the street.

The discussion turned to politics. At that time, an extreme right-wing party known as the Vlaams Belang had become popular among the Belgian working class. Vlaams Belang tapped into deep feelings of resentment in the Belgian people against the immigrants who came to Belgium from Turkey and Morocco. These immigrants often refused to integrate into Belgian society to any significant degree, forming separate Islamic communities that clashed with Belgian law and culture. Like most white, European families, the birth rate of the Belgians was well below replacement rate, while the birth rate in the Islamic communities was quite high. As Belgians saw the demographics of their nation shifting in the direction of the Islamic immigrants, some became very fearful and resentful.

The right wing in Belgium is quite different from the right wing in the United States. Generally speaking, the Republican Party in the United States simply does not have racist roots, especially when compared to the Democratic Party. The Republican Party of the United States led the fight against slavery. A higher percentage of Republican legislators than Democratic legislators voted for the 1964 Civil Rights Act. Today, a large portion of Republican "right wingers" would identify as evangelical Christians who reject racism in any form.

In Europe, things are a bit different. Some of the right wing parties of Europe really do have racist, neo-Nazi roots. Some of the founders of these parties were actually Nazi sympathizers during World War II. This was the case of the Vlaams Belang.

My farmer neighbor was a strong supporter of Vlaams Belang. When I questioned him about the racist roots of the party, he became quite agitated. He told me I didn't know anything about Vlaams Belang. He told me the party wasn't racist. He insisted that it was simply a party that worked for the good of the Belgian people.

Several hours passed, and my neighbor drank more than a few beers. As he loosened up, he began to talk about the topic that really upset him more than any other. During World War II, thousands of Belgians collaborated with the Nazis. Some joined Nazi SS units that were responsible for the war's worst atrocities. Now, many years later, the Belgian government was refusing to pay out government pensions for Belgian retirees who had fought in Nazi SS units. This great injustice deeply angered my neighbor.

WHAT CAUSES DO YOU SUPPORT?
There are many causes in this world. The causes that you choose to support say quite a lot about you. If the thing that upsets you the most is the fact that some old Nazi SS soldiers are not being paid their pensions, you might be a neo-Nazi.

What are the causes that the Mennonite church supports? The answer to that question reveals much about this church.

On the issue of terrorism and genocide, there is one community in this world that is more supportive of terrorism and genocide than any other. This community openly declares its support for terrorists and terrorist tactics. When polls are taken, well over fifty percent of this community routinely declares their support for acts of terrorism against civilians. The same polls reveal that this community does not desire to make peace with its enemies but would prefer to murder men, women and children with acts of terror.

This community celebrates terrorists. Squares and schools and streets are named after terrorists who were successful in murdering civilians.

The government of this community pays lifetime salaries to successful terrorists. A terrorist who managed to murder several children will likely receive a lifetime salary from the government that is greater than the salary the government pays one of its civil servants.

Thousands of members of this community literally celebrated in the streets on 9/11, as news spread that thousands of Americans had been murdered in a terrorist attack.[11]

When elections are held, this community usually votes for terrorist groups to be its leaders.

Children in this community are often taught that the noblest deed they can perform with their life is to become terrorists.

The target of this community's hatred is the same as the Nazis. This community hates the Jews of Israel with a genocidal passion. This community blames the Jews for every negative thing that takes place in this world. This community, of course, is that of the Palestinians.

PALESTINIANS AND TERRORISM

There is no community on the face of this earth that is more dedicated to terrorism and genocide than the Palestinians. They have proven this repeatedly with both words and deeds.

The Palestinian Authority (PA) actually pays generous salaries to the families of suicide bombers and imprisoned terrorists. The families

---

[11] http://www.foxnews.com/story/2001/09/12/arafat-horrified-by-attacks-but-thousands-palestinians-celebrate-rest-world.html

of imprisoned terrorists receive payments of $350 to $3,100 every month. The larger payments go to terrorists who have been convicted of more grievous crimes against Jews and have been imprisoned for longer periods of time. The families of suicide bombers who died in the act of terrorism receive payments of $350 per month. These payments made to terrorists' families can actually be higher than the salaries paid by the PA to civil servants.

In fact, about ten percent of the Palestinian Authority's budget is given to the families of terrorists, amounting to yearly payments of more than 300 million dollars. Palestinians are subsidized on a per capita basis at a higher rate than any other community on earth. Much of the Palestinian Authority's 4.2-billion-dollar budget is provided by donor countries, including various European nations and the USA. In effect, Europe and America help pay the salaries of these terrorists. The payments to terrorist families are represented to donor countries as "government salaries."

The Palestinians' commitment to terrorism can hardly be overstated. Terrorists are celebrated in Palestine. Streets and parks are named after terrorists. When a "successful" terrorist attack takes place in which Jewish civilians are murdered, the Palestinians rejoice. Celebrations are held on the streets of the Gaza Strip and the West Bank. Candy is handed out to the children.

Palestinian children are indoctrinated to believe that the highest calling on their lives is to murder Jews. They are taught this basic life message in schools, in camps, and on children's TV shows. They are taught that "martyrdom is better than peace." They are taught that "it is a Muslim's duty to kill Jews." They sing songs that glorify terrorist violence and martyrdom.

In fact, something resembling a death cult has taken shape in the Gaza Strip and West Bank. Terrorists and suicide bombers are the heroes here. The terrorist organization Hamas actually wins elections in these territories. Public opinion polls have repeatedly proven that well over half of Palestinian people openly support terrorism against Jewish civilians. There is little doubt that if the Palestinians are given the opportunity, they will act upon their threats to destroy Israel.

Of course, not every Palestinian feels this way. Some Palestinians truly desire to live at peace with their neighbors. Unfortunately, the polls indicate that this group is a minority and that the majority of Palestinians are deeply committed to terror and genocide.

RELENTLESS HATRED

It is difficult to exaggerate the Palestinians hatred for the Jews. Shlomi Eldar, an Israeli journalist and filmmaker was shocked and devastated when he realized just how deep this hatred went. Eldar heard a story about a newborn Palestinian child, Mohammed Abu, who was born without an immune system. Mohammed's only hope was to have a bone marrow transplant in an Israeli hospital. The transplant cost $55,000 USD.

This story touched Eldar's heart, and he was able to broadcast the need on Israeli television. An Israeli man who had lost his son in the Israel-Palestinian conflicts donated the $55,000 so that Mohammed Abu's life could be saved. The Palestinian baby received the treatment, and his life was saved.

Eldar made a video documentary of the whole story called "Precious Life." During the filming, he became friends with Mohammed's Palestinian Mother, Raida. In Eldar's documentary, Raida shared her feelings with the world. Instead of being overjoyed that her son's life had been saved, she insisted that life meant nothing. She declared that although the Israelis loved life, the Palestinians loved death. She declared her hope that one day Mohammed would grow up to become a suicide bomber.

Eldar was shocked. He recounted, "My first reaction was to stop filming. If the Israelis are helping this baby and he becomes a suicide bomber, what does this mean for our future? I was so disappointed….His mother wants to raise him as a suicide bomber!"[12]

If a woman who had received so much generosity from Israelis would sacrifice the life of her son to see a few of them murdered, then the hatred of the Palestinians is implacable indeed. If anything, the hatred of the Palestinians against the Jews seems to be even greater than the hatred that the Nazis had for the Jews. Which Nazi was willing to sacrifice his own child in hopes of murdering a few Jews? There are numerous videos of Palestinian mothers rejoicing over the deaths of their children as suicide bombers.

THE SOURCE OF PALESTINIAN RAGE

The Palestinians trace their rage back to the events surrounding the 1948 Israeli War, in which Israel defeated both the Palestinians and the armies of four Arab nations. The Jews had just passed through immeasurable suffering in the Holocaust, and many believed that the only answer for their situation was to form a new nation in the land of their fathers. Events were set in motion to reform the state of Israel, the first Jewish state in 2,000 years.

In November 1947, the UN General Assembly voted 33-13 to approve a partition plan that would divide Palestine into two independent Jewish and Arab states. The Jews of Israel celebrated the vote while the Arabs were enraged. A civil war immediately broke out between Arab and Jewish communities in Israel.

During this civil war, atrocities were committed by both sides, as hundreds of civilians were murdered by Jews and Palestinians alike. The Jews were in a more desperate situation than the Palestinians as they were fighting for their very survival. Their back was against the wall, and they had nowhere to flee. In contrast, the Palestinians could easily flee to nearby Arab dominated areas. There they could wait for

---

[12] www.foxnews.com/entertainment/2011/.../precious-life-suicide-bomber-shlomi-edar.htm

the Arab armies of the surrounding nations to invade Israel, allowing the Palestinians to reclaim their land. And so as the fighting approached Palestinian villages in Israel, thousands of Palestinians packed their belongings and fled. Some left in fear for their lives, while others simply did not want to live under Jewish control. Many thought that they would soon be able to return.

Israel won the civil war, and David Ben-Gurion declared Israel's statehood in May 14, 1948. Immediately after his announcement, the combined military forces of Iraq, Syria, Jordan, and Egypt invaded the new nation with the express purpose of destroying it. There was no talk of a "two state solution." The Arab armies were playing for keeps, desiring to crush the new state and bring the area completely under Arab control. Azzam Pasha, the General Secretary of the Arab League, told reporters on May 20, 1948: "We are fighting for an Arab Palestine."

The four Arab armies invaded Israel from all sides. The fighting lasted for ten months. Although vastly outnumbered and outgunned, the Israeli forces were able to stop the Arab invasion and push them back.

Israel kept control of the land allotted to it by the UN resolution, and took control of some of the land allotted by the UN to the Palestinians. Palestinians who had fled their villages as the fighting approached were no longer able to return. About 700,000 Palestinians became refugees. Palestinians today refer to their flight from Israel as Al-Nakba (the catastrophe).

Meanwhile, during the three years following the war, thousands of Jews living in Europe and the Middle East also became refugees. Many were expelled by Arabs infuriated at the creation of a Jewish state. About 700,000 Jews fled their homelands and resettled in Israel.

RESETTLING THE REFUGEES
Under normal circumstances, refugees are quickly resettled and assimilated into new communities. The UN refugee resettlement programs work to ensure that nobody lives in a refugee camp for more than a few years. The Jewish refugees who fled to Israel from Middle

Eastern nations were rapidly resettled and assimilated into Israel. They became Israelis.

Since 1948, there have been more than 60,000,000 refugees created by various conflicts around the world. Palestinian refugees actually represent less than one percent of all the refugees that have been created by the world's conflicts during the past 70 years. Under normal circumstances, the Arab nations that surrounded Israel would have assimilated the Palestinian refugees within a matter of months. They speak the same language and have the same background as their Arab neighbors. There was absolutely nothing that would have kept them from getting jobs and starting new lives in the Arab nations. If such a small nation as Israel could so rapidly assimilate 700,000 Jewish refugees, the 22 Arab nations, with over 100 times the population of Israel and over 600 times the land mass could have easily assimilated 700,000 Palestinian refugees.

Something very strange happened in the case of the Palestinian refugees. Seventy years later, many of the Palestinian refugees are still living in refugee camps. Their numbers are not decreasing; they are increasing. Today there are approximately 5.3 million Palestinian refugees including 1,603,018 who still live in the refugee camps. These camps are located in the West Bank and the Gaza Strip, also in Jordan, Lebanon, Syria, and Egypt.

With the exception of Jordan, the Arab countries that surround Israel have refused to give the Palestinian refugees full citizenship. Palestinians lack basic economic and political rights in these nations. They are restricted in their rights to work, vote, and own property. The Arab nations do not want to integrate the Palestinians. They prefer to keep them in the camps as a political weapon that can be used against Israel.

UNITED NATIONS CREATES A PERMANENT CRISIS
The United Nations High Commission for Refugees (UNHCR) is an organization that was created to deal with refugee crises around the

world. This organization is trained to resettle refugees as quickly as possible. But in the case of the Palestinian refugees, the UNHCR worked with the Arab nations to turn the Palestinian refugee issue into an unending crisis by creating permanent communities of refugees at Israel's borders.

The UN has created its own organization to deal with the Palestinian situation, the United Nations Relief Work Agency (UNRWA). This organization has a yearly budget of over a billion dollars. It is actually the largest agency in the United Nations. It employs 30,000 people, most of whom are Palestinians.

And so today, at the borders of Israel, there are refugee camps sponsored by the UN. These camps have become permanent cities, seething with hatred against Israel. The number of refugees is always increasing. They are now ten times the size that they were following the war. The UN has decided that in the case of the Palestinian refugees, even the grandchildren and great grandchildren of the original refugees will be classified as refugees.

Why was such a refugee system developed? Why have the nations of the earth worked together to create an unending Palestinian refugee crisis?

Quite simply, the refugee situation of the Palestinians has been manipulated by the Arab nations and the UN to nurture hatred against Israel. By creating growing, hate-filled cities at Israel's border they have created a problem that is impossible for Israel to solve. If Israel agrees to a two-state solution in which the Palestinians are allowed to form their own, independent nation, the state that forms at Israel's border will be a state completely dedicated to terrorism and the destruction of Israel.

In fact, many Palestinian activists do not want a two-state solution. They do not want their own state that would exist peacefully beside the state of Israel. Many demand a one-state solution, in which the Palestinians would dominate a single state encompassing Israel and the Palestinian territories.

Palestinian activists are demanding the "right of return." Palestinians activists claim that the "right of return" is a sacred right. They demand that Palestinian refugees be given the exact lands owned by their ancestors in the land of Israel.

If Israel would grant the right of return to the Palestinians, they would not only be allowing the 700,000 original refugees to return., but they would need to open the doors for 5,300,000 Palestinian descendants of the original refugees, a group that will soon multiply to more than 10,000,000 people. This would mean the end of Israel as a democratic, Jewish state. If the rapidly growing population of more than 5 million Palestinians were added to the population of Israel, the Palestinians would soon control the outcome of Israeli elections. The Palestinians have already proven that they are willing to elect the worst leaders imaginable. When given the right to vote in the Gaza Strip, the Palestinians immediately elected the terrorist group Hamas to be their leaders. If Israel granted Palestinians the "right of return," it would quite simply lead to the end of Israel as a nation and the genocide of the Jewish citizens of Israel.

In short, Israel is placed in an unwinnable situation. The enemies of Israel have manipulated the Palestinian refugee crisis to create a situation that Israel can never solve. A two-state solution will inevitably lead to the creation of a terrorist state at Israel's borders. A single-state solution will lead to the destruction of Israel. The current situation involves incredible tension and insecurity, as Israeli forces try to keep a lid on the pot that is boiling in the West Bank and Gaza Strip. The enemies of Israel were unable to defeat Israel on the battlefield, but they have manipulated the Palestinian refugee crisis into something that they hope will eventually cause Israel's demise.

During the past few decades, Israeli leaders have acquiesced to the idea of a two-state solution to mitigate the Palestinian refugee problem, seeing it as the lesser evil in an array of bad options. Israeli leaders have offered to turn over authority in the West to the Palestinians in return for a Palestinian cessation and renunciation of terror tactics. The Palestinians have largely refused to do their part in the negotiations. Giving up terrorism seems simply too much to ask from them.

A VERY GENEROUS OFFER

At the Camp David Summit of 2000, Prime Minister Ehud Barak of Israel made an extraordinarily generous offer to Palestinian leader Yasser Arafat. Barak proposed a two-state solution to the Palestinian crisis in which the Palestinians would receive 92 percent of the West Bank, and 100 percent of the Gaza Strip. Barak offered to dismantle most of the Israeli settlements. He even offered to give the Palestinians sovereignty over the Muslim and Christians quarters of Jerusalem, and custodianship over the Temple Mount where the Dome of the Rock is located. Palestinian refugees could return to the new Palestinian state. A massive international aid program would ease the Palestinians rehabilitation.

Although he was being offered almost everything he supposedly wanted, Arafat refused to consider Barak's offer. He even refused to offer a counter offer. President Clinton was enraged. He banged on the table and shouted "You are leading your people and the region to a catastrophe!"

Arafat did not care. He left the Camp David accords and led the Palestinian people into war against Israel. In the Second Intifada, Palestinians began a campaign of suicide bombing that killed more than 1,000 Israelis. More than 3,000 Palestinians were also killed.

ISRAELI WITHDRAWAL FROM THE GAZA STRIP

By the year 2005, peace negotiations with the Palestinians had gone nowhere, largely due to Palestinian leaders refusing to make any concessions for the sake of peace. Nevertheless, Prime Minister Ariel Sharon decided to make a unilateral gesture that he hoped would improve the situations with the Palestinians. Sharon decided to withdraw Israeli forces from the Gaza Strip, turning over the area to the Palestinians. As a part of this withdrawal, 8,000 Jews were coerced to leave their homes in Gaza.

Why did Israeli citizens need to leave their homes when the Gaza Strip was turned over to the Palestinians? Everyone assumed that ethnic cleansing was necessary for areas ruled by Palestinians. Although Arabs live free lives as Israeli citizens in Israel, everyone knows what would happen if Jews tried to do the same thing in an area ruled by Palestinians. They would be slaughtered.

Israel's withdrawal from the Gaza Strip didn't bring peace to the Gaza Strip. During the elections of January 2006, the Palestinians of the Gaza Strip voted for Hamas to become their representatives. Hamas is a terrorist organization.

The Hamas charter states:

> Israel will exist and will continue to exist until Islam will obliterate it, just as it obliterated others before it (quotation from The Martyr, Imam Hassan al-Banna).

> There is no solution for the Palestinian question except through Jihad.

> Initiatives, proposals and international conferences are all a waste of time and vain endeavors.

> Hamas is uniquely Palestinian, and strives to raise the banner of Allah over every inch of Palestine.[13]

The charter also quotes the words of the prophet Mohammed in which he prophesies about the day when the Muslims will murder all the Jews: "The Day of Judgment will not come until Muslims fight the Jews, when the Jew will hide behind stones and trees. The stones and trees will say, 'O Muslim, O servant of God, there is a Jew behind me, come and kill him.'"[14]

Khalil Al Hayya, a senior Hamas official made the intentions of Hamas very clear: "[You] Zionists, you have no place on the land of Palestine

---

[13] http://www.mythsandfacts.org/conflict/statute-treaties/hamas_charter.htm
[14] Sahih Muslim Volume 7, Book 41, Hadith 6985

... we shall expel you from our land and we will fight against you [on the land]. We will kill you or expel you from it when you are submissive."

Obviously, a people that elects terrorists to be its leaders will not find peace. Although Hamas gained 74 out of 132 parliamentary seats in the 2006 elections, Fatah, a Palestinian terrorist organization, founded in 1956, with the aim of   destroying the state of Israel,   did not willingly relinquish control of the Palestinian Authority to them. A violent conflict broke out between Fatah and Hamas, leading to the deaths of hundreds of Palestinians.

As Hamas gained the upper hand over Fatah in the Gaza Strip, it stepped up its attacks on Israel. Between 2005 and 2007 Hamas released 2,700 Qassam rockets into Israel from the Gaza Strip. It also supported numerous terrorist attacks against Israel.

BATTLING THE TERRORISTS

On December 27, 2008, Israel responded with overwhelming force as Israeli troops invaded the Gaza Strip in Operation Cast Lead. For three weeks, the Israeli troops battled against Hamas militants. The Israeli soldiers went to great lengths to avoid civilian casualties, but the Hamas use of civilians as "human shields" caused a significant number of civilian casualties. In the end, more than 113 Israelis lost their lives in conflict-related casualties, together with 1,735 Palestinians.

After the invasion, the rocket attacks ceased for a time as Hamas regrouped. In 2010, 150 rockets were launched against Israel as Hamas restarted its aggression. In 2011, 680 rocket launches and mortar attacks were launched toward Israeli population centers. The largest of these rockets contained hundreds of pounds of explosives.

In 2014, Hamas prepared 6,000 rockets for war against Israel. The largest of these, the Iranian Fajr-5 contained a payload of more than 400 pounds of explosives. Hamas began to fire these rockets into Israel. Hamas operatives also kidnapped and eventually murdered three Israeli teenagers.

Following these provocations, Israeli troops again invaded the Hamas ruled Gaza Strip to stop the rocket launches and search for the Israeli teenagers. Operation Protective Edge turned into a seven-week conflict, causing the deaths of 73 Israelis and more than 2,000 Palestinians.

RESULTS OF CONCESSIONS

Every time that Israel has offered the Palestinians concessions of various types, Palestinians have responded with increased aggression. When Israel withdrew from the Gaza Strip, Palestinians responded by electing terrorists as their leaders. When Barak offered Arafat nearly everything for which he could have asked, Arafat responded by starting a campaign of suicide bombings targeting Israeli civilians, the Second Intifada.

It is impossible to make peace with people who are wholeheartedly committed to one's destruction. It is impossible to make peace with terrorists. Every time a hand is offered to them, they will use that hand to try to pull one down. Every concession that is offered will be interpreted as a sign of weakness.

ISRAELI RESTRAINT VS. HAMAS BRUTALITY

In the face of enemies who are deeply committed to Israel's destruction, Israel has shown remarkable restraint. Before invading the Gaza Strip, the Israelis warned Palestinian civilians to leave the area they were planning to attack, using phone calls, TV and radio broadcasts, and leaflets. Their efforts to avoid harming civilians greatly exceeded the efforts that the United States has taken to avoid civilian casualties in its wars in Iraq and Afghanistan.

Hamas, on the other hand, did everything in its power to keep Palestinian civilians in the combat zone. Hamas uses Palestinian civilian casualties as a weapon against Israel. When Palestinian civilians die, Hamas spokesmen and the media immediately begin accusing Israel of genocide. The international community parrots Hamas and starts pressuring Israel to stop its attack.

Of course, Israel has never committed genocide against the Palestinians. The Palestinian population is not being reduced by Israel; it has actually grown more than 100 percent since 1970. Even while Israel was invading the Gaza Strip, it allowed hundreds of trucks carrying food and medicine to enter Gaza to feed the civilian population.

CONDEMNING ISRAEL

In every conflict between Israel and the Palestinians, the United Nations responds in exactly the same way, with condemnations of Israel. For example, between 2006 and 2016 the United Nations Human Rights Council adopted 135 resolutions criticizing various countries for human rights abuses. Sixty-eight of those resolutions were targeted against Israel. Between 2012 through 2015, the United Nations General Assembly has adopted a total of 97 resolutions criticizing various countries: 83 out of those 97 resolutions have been against Israel. The United Nations Security Council has passed 226 resolutions relating to Israel since 1948. Nearly all of them are critical of Israel.

Even the World Health Organization singles out Israel for condemnation, blaming Israel for the squalid conditions of the Palestinian refugee camps. And the United Nations Educational, Scientific, and Cultural Organization (UNESCO) passes about ten resolutions every year condemning Israel. If there is one thing that the United Nations is united about, it is condemning Israel.

This condemnation of Israel is usually led by the Arab nations that are extremely resentful of the fact that a Jewish state exists in the Middle East. The nations leading the condemnation of Israel are rarely democratically governed nations that respect the rights and freedoms of their citizens. In fact, Israel is probably the most democratic nation of the Middle East, the land that most protects the rights and freedoms of its citizens, including its Arab citizens.

In spite of this fact, the nations of the earth routinely unite to condemn Israel for the problem of the Palestinian refugees, a situation that the Arab nations have largely created by refusing to assimilate Palestinian refugees. The extreme hypocrisy of these condemnations is mind-boggling.

The truth is, every nation and tribe exists on land that has been taken by force from other nations and tribes. This is the human condition. In America, we drove out the Native Americans, the British, the French, and the Spaniards to take possession of our land. Before that, the Native American tribes lived in near constant warfare with one another. In the early 1800's, the Comanche drove out many tribes from present-day New Mexico and West Texas to form Comancheria. The Iroquois confederacy crushed the tribes of the eastern woodlands to form their empire.

The Spaniards defeated the Aztecs and the Incas. As they defeated those empires, they had lots of help from other Native American tribes that had been crushed and enslaved by the Aztecs and the Incas. There was a time when Shaka Zulu crushed the tribes of Southern Africa, slaughtering millions of people and combining the survivors into the Zulu tribe. White settlers eventually defeated the Zulu.

In fact, if you study the history of any nation, you will discover times in history when that nation rose up and dominated its neighbors, and times when that nation's neighbors dominated it. Nearly every nation in Europe had a "golden age" during which it dominated other nations. There was a time when Spain conquered much of the world before being defeated by stronger nations. There was a time when the Turks conquered much of the world as the Ottoman Empire spread across the earth, before falling apart in World War I. There was a time when Japan conquered much of the Far East. There were times when the Mongol armies crushed most of Asia and beyond with extreme brutality. And so on.

It is impossible to try and settle all the wrongs of history. The best thing that nations can do is to make the best of the situation that history and circumstance have dealt them. Nations that feed upon bitterness become poisoned and capable of committing great atrocities. Nations that humble themselves and turn to the Lord receive much grace. The nations that condemn Israel for its sins have usually committed much greater sins in their own history.

GOD'S PLAN FOR ISRAEL

In light of the fact that almost every nation has a very bloody history, why do the nations unite to condemn Israel? Why do the nations work to create terrorist states at Israel's borders? After millions of Jews were slaughtered in the Holocaust of the 20th century, why do nations continue to hate the Jews so much?

The Father of Lies rules over the nations. The Father of Lies knows that God has awesome plans for the nation of Israel. He knows that when God's purposes for the land of Israel are fulfilled, His purposes for the earth will also be fulfilled. In response to that plan, the Evil One has stirred up an incredible level of hatred against the Jews.

There is no fundamental difference between the hatred that is found in anti-Zionism and the hatred that is found in anti-Semitism. It is the same hatred, taking two different forms. The hatred that lives in the hearts of the Palestinians is the same hatred that filled Nazi Germany. The spirit that inspires this hatred is the devil himself.

It is the Lord who has reestablished the nation of Israel after 2,000 years. It is the Lord who reestablished Israel so that He can fulfill his promises for this nation. The Evil One hates the nation of Israel for this very reason.

> **For this is what the Sovereign Lord says: I myself will search for my sheep and look after them. As a shepherd looks after his scattered flock when he is with them, so will I look after my sheep. I will rescue them from all the places where they were scattered on a day of clouds and darkness. I will bring them out from the nations and gather them from the countries, and I will bring them into their own land. I will**

pasture them on the mountains of Israel, in the ravines and in all the settlements in the land" (Ezekiel 34 11-13).

The modern-day nation of Israel represents only a partial fulfillment of God's promises for Israel. He has brought the Jews back to their land. However, this nation has not yet received their Messiah. The modern nation of Israel is a secular, humanistic nation. When they win victories over the Arabs, they do not give God the glory.

You can compare the modern nation of Israel to the valley of dry bones described in Ezekiel 37. The dry bones have been brought together, but the holy nation has not yet come alive. The Lord will breathe upon these bones, and they will live. There are many biblical prophecies of the day when Israel will turn wholeheartedly to the Lord. These prophecies will be fulfilled. The Lord will cause the secular, rebellious nation of Israel to become a holy nation. He will bring Israel back to Himself.

"Why do the nations rebel and the peoples plot in vain?" (Psalm 2:1 HCSB). Why do they become so enraged against the plans and purposes of God? The nations rage and rebel because they think that they are God. They think that they are the ones who determine the course of human history. They think that they are able to bring forth peace while rebelling against the Prince of Peace.

The complete foolishness of the nations will be revealed in these times. The rebellion and evil of the nations will be revealed. As it is manifested, whose side do the Christians choose? Is the church able to recognize what the Spirit of the Lord is doing and support it? Or does the church join with the nations to condemn and oppose what God is doing?

THE CHURCH CONDEMNS ISRAEL

Many Christian denominations are joining with the Palestinians in their cause against Israel. Even though the Palestinians clearly announce their intentions to destroy Israel, and even though the Palestinians have backed up their words with actions at every possible opportunity,

Christians still think that the state of Israel is the obstacle to peace in the Middle East. They think that if Israel would just withdraw from the disputed territories, peace would be the result. They do not consider the fact that every time Israel has made concessions to the Palestinians, the Palestinians have responded with more murder and outrage than before.

On Mennonite college campuses, one of the most popular causes pitting an oppressed group against its oppressor is the cause of the Palestinians. In the name of peace, Mennonite college students throw their support behind the Palestinian cause. In the name of peace, they condemn every defensive action of the state of Israel, as they defend and excuse the murderous deeds of the Palestinians.

How can Christians be so blind? Can liberal Christians really not tell the difference between a soldier who fights to protect his nation and a terrorist? Can they really not tell the difference between an Israeli soldier and a member of Hamas? Can they discern no moral difference between the two?

This moral blindness is shocking and evil. It is a sign that churches have become so hijacked by the enemy that they can no longer tell good from evil. Good is called evil, and evil is called good.

Christian organizations make documentaries about Israel and the Palestinians in which they paint the Israelis as cruel monsters and the Palestinians as the peace-loving victims of Israeli aggression. One such documentary entitled "Children of the Nakba" was made by the Mennonite Central Committee. These documentaries talk of the great suffering that Palestinians undergo at the Israeli checkpoints, without ever explaining why those checkpoints are necessary for Israel's survival. They talk of Palestinian homes being bulldozed, without explaining that the homes that are being bulldozed are the homes of suicide bombers and other terrorists. They mourn the construction of the wall that Israel has built without explaining why that wall is so necessary. They do not speak about how deeply committed the Palestinians are to terrorism and the destruction of Israel. They do not talk about how frequently the Palestinians have acted upon their beliefs. They don't mention the fact that if Israel withdraws from the West Bank, the West bank will surely come under the complete control of a terrorist organization just as the Gaza Strip has.

The Mennonite Church USA has proposed a resolution on Israel-Palestine that delegates will vote to approve at their convention in Orlando Florida in July, 2017. The resolution calls upon Mennonites to "confess and lament" their sin of embracing or tolerating Christian Zionist theology. Christian Zionist theology is defined as believing that God has gathered together the Jews in the state of Israel before the second coming of Christ, and that Christians should support the state of Israel.

The resolution makes an attempt to be unbiased and evenhanded in its approach to the Israeli-Palestinian conflict Israelis and Palestinians. Nevertheless, each point of action is designed to use economic and political pressure to coerce Israel to give in to Palestinian demands.

The resolution calls upon Mennonites to boycott companies that are associated with Israel's occupation of the West Bank, and to boycott products that are produced by Jews living in the West Bank. The resolution states, "We want to invest in peace with justice, not profit or benefit from the suffering of others."

The resolution supports measures to end Israel's occupation of the West Bank and to freeze Israeli settlements in areas claimed by the Palestinians. It calls upon the US government to end arms sales to the Israelis.

Out of all the injustice in this world, out of all the atrocities, the Mennonites choose to take up the cause of the Palestinians in the Israel-Palestinian conflict. No resolution has been made about the genocide being committed against Christians by ISIS. No resolution is being passed concerning the civil war in Syria or the fact that Arabs living in Arab nations have few political rights. The injustice that demands a resolution to be passed is the injustice committed by the Israelis against the Palestinians.

SUPPORTING THE ENEMY'S AGENDA

The causes people choose to support say quite a lot about them, just as it did with my Belgian neighbor.   It would be difficult to find two causes that are more completely against the purposes of God than the cause of gay marriage and the cause of the Palestinians against Israel. These are the two causes that a large part of the Mennonite Church is choosing to support.

In supporting gay marriage, persons rebel against the very foundational principles of creation. God created mankind in his image; male and female he created them. He said, **"It is not good that man should be alone; I will make him a helper comparable to him"** (Genesis 2:18) **For this reason, a man "shall leave his father and mother and be joined to his wife, and they shall become one flesh"** (Genesis 2:24).

The devil has a purpose to blur every distinction that God has created, to twist and pervert everything that God has created. He desires to bring such confusion, darkness and evil upon a society that men "no longer know their right hand from their left."   In this state of confusion, men are easily manipulated by the powers of darkness. They become so rebellious against everything that is good and pure that they call evil good, and good evil.

Gay marriage is a part of this fundamental perversion. The force that is pushing the acceptance and celebration of gay marriage into every corner of American society is not the Holy Spirit. It is another spirit entirely. It is the spirit of the world, the God of this age, who is the spiritual force behind these abominations. **"The god of this age has blinded the minds of unbelievers, so that they cannot see the light of the gospel that displays the glory of Christ, who is the image of God"** (II Corinthians 4:4). **"Now we have received not the spirit of the world, but the Spirit who is from God, that we might understand the things freely given us by God"** (I Corinthians 2:12).

Likewise, God has a purpose and a plan for his people Israel that is revealed throughout Scripture.   What right does the Mennonite

Church have to call for believers to "confess and lament" the fact that they believed those promises?

The Apostle Paul spent much of his life suffering under the persecution brought by religious Jews. Nevertheless, he saw the plan of God for this nation. He saw that the spiritual blindness that was upon Israel was a temporary blindness, a blindness that would remain until "the fullness of the Gentiles has come in."

Romans 11:25-27 says:

> **For I do not desire, brethren, that you should be ignorant of this mystery, lest you should be wise in your own opinion, that blindness in part has happened to Israel until the fullness of the Gentiles has come in.**
>
> **And so all Israel will be saved, as it is written: "THE DELIVERER WILL COME OUT OF ZION, AND HE WILL TURN AWAY UNGODLINESS FROM JACOB; FOR THIS IS MY COVENANT WITH THEM, WHEN I TAKE AWAY THEIR SINS."**

Now as we approach the end of this age and the time of final harvest, the fullness of the Gentiles is being brought in. As that takes place, Israel herself will turn to the Lord and receive her Messiah.

THE HIJACKING OF THE MENNONITE CHURCH

What can be said about a church that believes that the Holy Spirit is leading it to support the cause of gay marriage and the cause of the Palestinians against Israel? Such a church shakes an angry fist at God as they oppose His plans and the laws of His creation.

It can only be said that this church has been hijacked by deceiving spirits. This church might talk about obeying the Holy Spirit of God, but it is obeying an evil spirit. Its guiding light, its "North Star", is no longer the Spirit of Christ.

What led to this hijacking? To sum up the previous chapters: under the influence of Yoder and other Anabaptist scholars, campus Christians stopped emphasizing individual salvation, the reconciliation between God and man that is made possible by the cross of Jesus

Christ. Yoder and others claimed that the main point of the cross of Christ was not that it was a sacrifice for sin, but that it represented Christ's refusal to use violence as He clashed with the powers ruling society. They concluded that Christians follow Christ's example as they refuse to participate in government sanctioned violence such as war and the death penalty.

As individual salvation was de-emphasized, peace and pacifism took a central place in the Mennonite church. Mennonites formed close ties with leftists and atheists who supported peace and pacifism, as they pulled away from conservative evangelicals. In time, the liberal wing of the Mennonite church began to embrace every left wing, politically correct cause imaginable as it was hijacked by the spirit of the age. Today the Mennonite church supports the Palestinians hate-filled jihad against Israel in the name of peace, and many of its leaders and members support gay marriage in the name of love.

In the days ahead, the resolutions and teachings that flow out of the hijacked Mennonite colleges and institutions will be increasingly antichrist in nature. In God's time, these religious institutions will be severely judged. Mennonite colleges and universities that teach students to rebel against the Lord will soon close their doors. Judgment begins in the house of the Lord (I Peter 4:17).

5 THE HIJACKER

THE CUCKOO BIRD

In Europe, there is a bird known as the cuckoo. The cuckoo bird makes the distinctive cuckoo sound that old, pendulum-driven cuckoo clocks imitate as they strike the hours. The bird that inspired the sound of these clocks is quite an interesting bird indeed.

The cuckoo is what is known as a brood parasite. The mother cuckoo does not build a nest of her own. She looks for the nest of another bird and lays her egg inside of it. The egg hatches, and the young cuckoo takes over the nest.

In simple words, the cuckoo is a hijacker. It always attempts to hijack the nest of another bird and make it its own. The amazing thing is, it not only hijacks the nest, it also hijacks the parents. When a cuckoo chick takes over a nest, the birds that built that nest for their own offspring willingly feed and raise the cuckoo chick instead.

The appearance of the cuckoo egg depends upon which group of female cuckoos it comes from. Female cuckoos are divided into "gentes," groups of female cuckoos that target different species of birds with their deception. For example, one group of female cuckoos lays blue eggs that mimic the blue eggs of the redstart. Another group of female cuckoos lays eggs that resemble the eggs of the reed warbler. Another group targets the dunnocks.

Cuckoos are remarkably adapted for a life of deception. The adult cuckoos are grey with barred feathers on their underbelly. A female cuckoo looks remarkably like a sparrow hawk. So, when a female cuckoo approaches the nest of a reed warbler, this deception provides the mother just enough time to complete her business. The reed warblers are intimidated by the "sparrow hawk," and instead of chasing the intruder away, they abandon their nests for a few minutes.

The female cuckoo lays her egg in the reed warbler's nest. The egg matches the colors and markings of the reed warbler's eggs. It is slightly larger than the reed warbler's eggs, with a thicker shell that allows it to be quickly dropped into a strange nest without cracking.

As part of the cuckoo's deception, the female cuckoo always casts one reed warbler egg from the nest as she lays her own egg. Thus the number of eggs in the nest remains the same, and the reed warbler is less likely to recognize the deception and reject the cuckoo egg.

The reed warblers are moderately successful at recognizing cuckoo eggs. About 20 percent of the female reed warblers realize that something has happened, and these abandon the nest to build another. Another 12 percent recognize the egg of the cuckoo and cast it out of the nest. The others sit on their nests as if nothing has happened, and the deception succeeds. The cuckoo egg usually hatches before the other eggs of the bird who built the nest because the cuckoo embryo is more highly developed than the embryo of other birds; therefore, the eggs hatch more quickly.

After about 12 days, the cuckoo chick hatches, blind and bald. This chick is born with a unique inner drive: from the moment it is born, it has a compelling urge to murder everyone sharing its nest.

And so, the cuckoo chick, less than 24 hours old, blind and naked, does everything in its power to cast the eggs of the reed warbler out of the nest. It strives with all of its effort to scoop the eggs up onto its back. The cuckoo chick actually has a depression in the center of its back where it balances the egg. Then it hoists the warbler egg up to the wall of the nest where it heaves the egg over the side as it totters on the edge of the nest. The egg splatters on the ground. The cuckoo chick rests a few minutes before it does the same thing with the other eggs.

If the reed warbler eggs have already hatched, the cuckoo chick treats the hatchlings the same way that it treats the eggs. It scoops them up on its back and then pushes them up over the edge of the nest where they fall to the ground and die.

The single-minded purpose of the blind, flailing cuckoo chick is an amazing thing to see. The eyes of this chick have not yet been opened. It has never been taught anything in life. Its drive to murder its siblings is something with which it is born.

Once the chick has succeeded in killing its siblings, it completely hijacks the nest. An adult cuckoo grows to about 13 inches in length, about three times the size of a reed warbler. In order to grow to its adult size quickly, it needs all the food that its adopted parents can gather.

The reed warbler parents are unable to resist the cries of the hungry cuckoo chick. They gather all the insects and spiders that they can find to feed their adopted child. The cuckoo chick gives a rapid begging call that sounds like an entire brood of reed warbler chicks. The constant cries motivate the parents to continually feed the chick.

In this way, the cuckoo chick grows quickly. Within just two weeks, it is about three times the size of the adult reed warblers that are feeding it. It is a strange sight to see the tiny reed warblers feeding the adopted, fratricidal cuckoo chick as it tries to balance on the tiny nest looking like a small, scruffy chicken. The reed warblers continue to feed the cuckoo even after it leaves the nest.

As summer comes to an end, the cuckoo begins its migration from Europe to Africa where it spends the winter. The following summer, it will return to the area of its birth as it attempts to hijack another bird's nest for its own offspring.

THE HIJACKER

The cuckoo bird represents the spirit that attempts to hijack every church, every school, and every religious institution in America. The name of this spirit is religion. The spirit of religion pretends to be the Spirit of God, but it is actually a manifestation of the Father of Lies, the devil himself.

Religion is the counterfeit, the fake. It might look like the real thing, but it has no real value. Religion is the shell without the substance. It is the appearance of righteousness without actual righteousness. It is talking about the love of God without actually having the love of God. It is talking about God and His ways without actually knowing God.

The sons of religion are the workers in the vineyard, who decide that the vineyard belongs to them. When the owner sends his representatives, they refuse to receive them. Some of them they beat, and some of them they kill. Finally, the owner sends his son, and they kill him (Luke 20:9-18).

The sons of religion are the tares in the field. They are similar in appearance to the wheat that is growing, but they will never produce a good harvest. They are the sons of the devil, not the sons of the kingdom (Matthew 13:24-43).

The offspring of religion mimic the children of God, but they are not the children of God. They were not born out of a true encounter with the living God. They are the product of religious men and the religious systems of men. They are born with a deep hatred for the true children of God, those who truly know God, who hear the voice of God, and follow Him. The sons of religion will attempt to drive out or destroy every true child of God from the organizations that they control.

When this spirit gains control of a religious institution, it always murders the spiritual babies. New Christians who attend a college that has been hijacked by religion will usually completely lose their faith while they are in college. New believers who encountered the living God will often lose their faith if they join a church that is dominated by the spirits of religion.

Just as a cuckoo chick takes ownership of the nest of a reed warbler, the sons of religion believe that they are the rightful owners of religious institutions. They believe that the churches belong to them, that the Christian schools belong to them, and that every religious organization is their rightful possession.

When religious men take control of an organization, that organization will never again be led by the Spirit of the Lord in a life-giving way. Religious men have an instinctive dislike, even a hatred, of those who are led by the Spirit of God. They are suspicious of those who are led by the Spirit of God. Religious men will make sure that anyone who hears and obeys the voice of God will be marginalized and pushed aside in their organization.

Religious men do everything in their power to ensure that the sons of God's kingdom are unable to rise up in the institutions that they control. They see that there are procedures in place that weed out the sons of God from having any real influence or authority. Perhaps they demand that employees in their organization have degrees from institutions that are controlled by religion. Those who graduate from those institutions are usually very religious by the time that they graduate.

Just as the cuckoo chick hijacks not only the nest but also the reed warbler parents, there are many people that end up serving religious systems instead of obeying the Spirit of God. Just as the cuckoo chick monopolizes all the resources of its adopted reed warbler parents, the spirit of religion monopolizes all the resources of the ones it hijacks.

Religious organizations monopolize the resources of American Christians. American Christians give enormous amounts of money to institutions that are dominated by religious spirits. They give large sums for the construction of church buildings that are controlled by religious men. They pay tens of thousands of dollars for their children to be educated in "Christian" colleges that have been completely hijacked by the spirit of religion. Unfortunately, this money does not advance the kingdom of heaven in any way. It advances the purposes of religion.

Like the cuckoo, the spirit of religion tries to create things that look like the real thing. The spirit of religion tries to imitate the Holy Spirit. The spirit of religion sounds very spiritual, with high-minded purposes and goals, and yet, the fruit of the spirit of religion is never the fruit of the kingdom of heaven. The fruit of the spirit of religion is always slavery.

Religion is a hijacker. The spirit of religion attempts to hijack every church, every school and every institution. When it hijacks these entities, they become vehicles for the kingdom of darkness instead of the kingdom of heaven.

THE RELIGION OF THE PHARISEES
Religion takes many different forms. In the time of Jesus, the spirit of religion worked through the Pharisees. On paper, the Pharisees seemed to believe many of the right things. They held many correct, biblical doctrines. In spite of the fact that their doctrines were often correct, the Pharisees were not led by the Spirit of God. They were led and controlled by a religious spirit.

It is possible to believe all the right doctrines about God and yet not know God. It is possible to know the written word without knowing the Living Word. It is possible to be a religious scholar who knows all the right answers to everything, and who yet has never encountered the living God, submitted one's heart, and said "yes" to Him.

The Pharisees thought they were the sons of God. They thought they were the true servants of God, the righteous ones that God would use to establish His kingdom. In fact, their hearts were far from God. They believed in many correct doctrines, but they did not actually love God or know Him.

These Pharisees hated and despised the true sons of the kingdom. They hated the Spirit of God and those who were led by the Spirit of God. They became the worst persecutors of the church of Jesus Christ. They thought they were serving God, but, in fact, they were only serving religion.

THE RELIGION OF ISLAM
One form that religion takes today is found in Islam. Religion works in a similar way in Islam as it did among the Pharisees. Deep in his heart, a religious, self-righteous Muslim feels superior to any pork-eating Christian. He is sure that his religious rituals and deeds are pleasing to God and that God despises non-Muslims just as much as he does. He is sure that if God wanted to use men to do His work, He would surely choose a religious Muslim such as himself. When this arrogant, self-righteous man is confronted by the true servants of God, he might well try to persecute them or even murder them, just as the Pharisees did to the servants of God in their day.

This religious arrogance was taught by Mohammed himself. A spirit spoke to Mohammed a revelation about the superiority of his followers: "You are the best of peoples, evolved for mankind, enjoining what is right, forbidding what is wrong, and believing in Allah" (Koran 3:110).

The spirit told Mohammed that the best people were those of his generation. The second best would be the following generation, and so forth down the line (Sahih Bukhari 6065).

The same spirit spoke to Mohammed about non-Muslims. They are diseased (Koran 2:10), perverted (Koran 2:99), stupid (Koran 2:171), and deceitful (Koran 3:73).

THE RELIGION OF POLITICAL CORRECTNESS
In America, a religion has developed on secular college campuses. It is a very bigoted, self-righteous, and judgmental religion. It is a religion that permanently condemns people for committing the smallest infractions of its legalistic code. For the purposes of this book, I will refer to this religion as the Religion of Political Correctness.

This religion has much in common with the left-wing campus Christianity described in chapters two and three of this book that has so deeply influenced liberal Mennonites. It is basically the same religion, except it is missing the Christianity part. The Religion of Political Correctness claims not to be religious at all.

Like the followers of left-wing campus Christianity, the Religion of Political Correctness divides people into two categories: the oppressors and the oppressed. The oppressors are the sinners, and the oppressed are the victims. White males are the ultimate oppressors. African Americans, Native Americans, women, gays, lesbians, and others are placed in the oppressed category. An oppressor can only be freed from his sinful state by repenting of his white privilege and joining the cause of the oppressed.

This religion allows no dissent on certain issues. It is not permissible to point out the failings of any ethnic group except white Americans. It is not permissible to stray from the orthodox view of climate change. It is not permissible to question the wisdom of sex change operations. It is certainly not permissible to question the fundamental right of gay marriage.

Any deviation from the orthodox views of the Politically Correct Religion are immediately labeled "hate speech" and "intolerance." Even the slightest deviation from the orthodoxy of this religion provokes an outpouring of self-righteous venom.

The Religion of Political Correctness claims to value "tolerance" above all other virtues. In fact, the social justice warriors who serve this religion are some of the most intolerant people on this planet. They are intolerant of those who believe that marriage is between a man and a woman. And they are intolerant of evangelical Christians in general. They would gladly see evangelical Christians completely driven out of any position of influence or authority in this nation. They celebrate seeing them lose their businesses and their jobs for the sin of disagreeing with their politically correct orthodoxy.

THE HIJACKING OF AMERICA'S TOP UNIVERSITIES
Like every other form of religion, the Religion of Political Correctness is a hijacker. The cuckoo birds of the Religion of Political Correctness have been successful in hijacking many of our nation's most esteemed educational institutions.

Harvard and Yale Universities are usually considered the most prestigious universities in America. Harvard University was founded in 1636 for the purpose of training Christian ministers. The original motto for Harvard University, adopted in 1692, was *Veritas Christo Ecclesiae* (Truth for Christ and the Church)."

Here is an excerpt from Harvard University's "Rules and Precepts" that were adopted in 1646:

> **Let every Student be plainly instructed, and earnestly pressed to consider well, the main end of his life and studies is, to know God and Jesus Christ which is eternal life (John 17:3) and therefore to lay Christ ... as the only foundation of all sound knowledge and learning. And seeing the Lord only giveth wisdom, Let everyone seriously set himself by prayer in secret to seek it of him" (Proverbs 2:3).**

This statement declares that the main purpose of a man's life and studies is to know God and Jesus Christ. It declares that Christ is the foundation of all sound knowledge and learning. True wisdom comes from God, and everyone should seek this true wisdom in prayer.

With these words, we can catch a glimpse of the original purpose of Harvard University. This institution was founded to raise up leaders who would truly know the living God and follow after Him. This university understood that the foundation of all knowledge is found in Jesus Christ, and that without Christ, everything else is meaningless and foolish.

Unfortunately, the cuckoo birds were able to enter Harvard University. They laid their eggs, and the sons of religion were able to hijack the nest. Today, Harvard University is very hostile toward biblical Christianity. It is no longer a place where Christ is recognized as the foundation of all sound knowledge. It is a place that has attempted to drive the knowledge of Christ out of science and education. Harvard University has become a temple for the Religion of Political Correctness -completely controlled by the cuckoo birds.

Eighty years after Harvard University was founded, a group of congregational ministers began to feel that Harvard was being hijacked from its original purpose. Sensing Harvard University was becoming too secular, these pastors found a wealthy sponsor who shared their concerns, Elihu Yale. With Elihu Yale's donation of $2,800, they formed Yale University in 1718. Yale's motto was *Lux et Veritas* (Truth and Light).

The pastors stated their objective in starting Yale University, that "Youth may be instructed in the Arts and Sciences who through the blessing of God may be fitted for Public employment both in Church and Civil State." Students were required to "live religious, Godly and blameless lives according to the rules of God's Word, diligently reading the Holy Scriptures, the fountain of light and truth; and constantly attend upon all the duties of religion, both in public and secret."

Just like the students of Harvard, the students at Yale were instructed to "...consider the main end of his study to know God in Jesus Christ."

Yale University seemed to succeed and stay on the right course for a number of years. More than 80 years after its founding, one of its faculty members wrote concerning the students, "It would delight your heart to see how the trophies of the cross are multiplied in this institution. Yale College is a little temple: prayer and praise seem to be the delight of the greater part of the students."

Unfortunately, today Yale University has become just another temple in the Religion of Political Correctness. Biblical Christianity is rejected at Yale, while every extreme left-wing cause is given a platform. At Yale's biennial Sex Week, the campus celebrates every kind of sexual perversion imaginable. Evangelical Christian voices are silenced and condemned.

THE ARROGANCE OF RELIGION

There are several characteristics that are always seen in a religious spirit, no matter what form that spirit takes. One of these characteristics is arrogance. With a religious spirit, there is always a sense of superiority, a sense of religious arrogance. This arrogance was repeatedly demonstrated by the Pharisees as they interacted with Jesus. The Pharisees believed that their religious training and position made them far superior to Jesus, the son of a carpenter who they believed was born out of wedlock. They said to Jesus, **"We were not born of fornication; we have one Father—God" (John 8:41)**. When they had the opportunity, they spit on Him and mocked Him (Mark 14:65).

They said to the man born blind who was healed by Jesus **"You were steeped in sin at birth; how dare you lecture us!"** (John 9:34)

Likewise, all who are bound by religion exhibit this same arrogance. Mohammed taught his followers that they were far superior to non-Muslims, that they should not become friends with non-Muslims: "O ye who believe! Fight those of the disbelievers who are near to you, and let them find harshness in you..." (Koran 9:123 Pickthal).

"Let not believers take disbelievers as allies rather than believers. And whoever [of you] does that has nothing with Allah, except when taking precaution against them in prudence. And Allah warns you of Himself, and to Allah is the [final] destination"(Koran 3:28).

Many Muslims will refuse even to shake hands with a non-Muslim, considering him to be unclean because of his habits of eating pork and petting dogs.

Most religious men are not so crude as Mohammed, who openly proclaimed that his followers were morally superior to all other men in all other ages. Most religious men hide their sense of superiority deep in their hearts while engaging in a show of humility on the outside. Yet the same basic arrogance can be found in the followers of every religion. They are not teachable. They are convinced they have all the answers. They are convinced that they are qualified to judge just about everybody.

MAN-MADE SYSTEMS OF RULES AND RIGHTEOUSNESS
Those who are led by a religious spirit always follow a man-made system of righteousness. Those who obey religion cannot have transformed hearts because they are not in relationship with the only One who can change men's hearts. Instead of seeing a true transformation of lives, the followers of religion follow a system of rules, a system of do's and don'ts by which they can prove their own

righteousness and rate the righteousness of others. The Pharisees had an extremely intricate system of rules and regulations that they followed. They didn't only follow the Law of Moses, they built up a system of man-made laws around each one of Moses' commandments. They judged men according to how well they kept these commandments. They condemned Jesus when He didn't obey their man-made system of rules.

Of course, this system of rules cannot change a man's heart. The Pharisees used this system of rules to justify themselves, but, in fact, their hearts did not change. Jesus said of the Pharisees, **"You are white-washed tombs, beautiful on the outside, on the inside full of dead men's bones and everything unclean"** (Matthew 23:27).

Likewise, Islam is a system of religious rules and regulations. Muslims use these rules to condemn everyone who doesn't obey them and to feel superior about themselves when they follow them.

For example, Muslims have very detailed rules regarding prayer. According to Mohammed's revelations, Allah counts the moments a Muslim spends in prayer, and he watches over the rituals of prayer to be sure that they are performed perfectly. Allah keeps a running tally of good deeds versus bad deeds. Good deeds cancel out sins. Allah keeps track of exactly how much time is spent in prayer and the preparations for prayer.

According to the following highly regarded Islamic hadith, the prayer offered in mosque has 25 times more value than a prayer offered in a man's house, if the one praying washes himself perfectly and performs the prayer perfectly. The angels pray for Allah's blessing and forgiveness upon that man the whole time he is in the mosque, either praying or waiting for the prayers to begin, just so long as he doesn't pass wind (yes, it really says that).

> The prayer offered in congregation is twenty-five times more superior (in reward) to the prayer offered alone in one's house or in a business center, because if one performs ablution and does it perfectly, and then proceeds to the mosque with the sole intention of praying, then for each step which he takes towards the mosque,

Allah upgrades him a degree in reward and (forgives) crosses out one sin till he enters the mosque. When he enters the mosque he is considered in prayer as long as he is waiting for the prayer and the angels keep on asking for Allah's forgiveness for him and they keep on saying: 'O Allah! Be Merciful to him, O Allah! Forgive him, as long as he keeps on sitting at his praying place and does not pass wind" (Bukhari 1:466).

Likewise, the Religion of Political Correctness has a long list of rules that must be followed to avoid condemnation. Every ethnic group must be referred to by a politically correct title. A black man must be referred to as an African-American, in spite of the fact that his ancestors might have been living in America far longer than the average white man's. Of course, a white man whose ancestors lived in Africa for four hundred years should not be called an African-American. Illegal aliens must be referred to as "undocumented immigrants." And so on. The terms continually change, and every student needs to keep current with the correct term, or he will be accused of hate and intolerance.

The student with male genitalia that believes he is a woman must be referred to as "she", even if "she" wears a beard. The student with female genitalia that feels like a man must be referred to as "he" in spite of "his" monthly periods. Anyone who deviates from using the correct pronoun is guilty of hate speech.

There is an acceptable, politically correct way of talking about every topic and an acceptable, politically correct viewpoint on each topic. These acceptable views can change overnight. One day it was acceptable for Barack Obama himself to oppose gay marriage, and the next everybody needed to support gay marriage or face the consequences.

"TOLERANCE" ISN'T LOVE

Political correctness is just a bunch of rules that America's liberal elites use to condemn those who disagree with them. The speech codes and other religious rules in the Religion of Political Correctness have nothing to do with real righteousness, or with the content of person's heart. Even if you a man uses all the proper, politically correct words for each "oppressed".

For example, in this book, I refuse to obey the speech codes of political correctness when I speak about Islam. Islam is not a religion of peace. Islam is a violent religion that blocks multitudes from the grace of God.

The disciples of political correctness will undoubtedly accuse me of hate speech and Islamophobia because I refuse to adhere to the politically correct fictions regarding Islam. If I refuse to speak about Islam in a way that would be acceptable to the disciples of political correctness, does that mean that I hate Muslims? Of course not. I work with many missionaries who spend hours every day praying for Muslims and preaching the gospel to them. We pray for God to fill our hearts with supernatural love for Muslims. You might even say that we love Muslims so much that we are willing to give our lives for them, to reach them with the gospel of Jesus Christ.

I can't judge what is in a man's heart, but it is possible that we love Muslims more than the disciples of political correctness do. If I one day give my life preaching the gospel to Muslims so that they can be saved, it is okay with me. I know that the African missionaries that I work with feel the same way.

Likewise, I am sure that I will be accused of homophobia because of the politically incorrect teachings in the first chapter of this book. If you speak the truth about homosexual sin, does that mean that you hate or fear homosexuals? Of course not.

Who truly loves homosexuals? The one who affirms them in their sin and refuses to speak the truth to them? The person bound by political correctness who is afraid of speaking anything that might offend a member of one of the "oppressed" groups? Do these people demonstrate the love of God?

The parents who pray day and night for the salvation of their son who has chosen a homosexual lifestyle demonstrate real love. They love their child deeply, and they speak the truth to him with deep conviction. They love him so much that they are willing even to offend him if it will result in his salvation.

The ministries that actually believe that homosexuals can change and work to help them change are demonstrating real love. They are paying a high price as they share the love of Christ with homosexuals. They are accused of homophobia and hatred as they speak the truth in love. They are hated and despised by much of society, but they don't let ridicule and persecution stop them from helping those who desperately need help.

Very few people are willing to pay such a price. It is so much easier to just be "tolerant" and pretend that everything is fine as multitudes walk a road leading to destruction. May God bless, strengthen, and encourage those ministries so that they will not falter and become discouraged.

May God give much grace to those who have decided to repent and leave the homosexual lifestyle. May they walk in victory and power, as they demonstrate the complete victory of Christ over all sin. They will be mocked, hated and despised by those who insist that change is impossible, but they will be highly honored for eternity.

If your young child is playing on a street, oblivious to a truck that is barreling towards him, should you affirm and encourage that child, or scream at him? If you love that child, you will scream at him, and do everything in your power to push him off the road so that he is not struck by the truck. Likewise, those who love deeply will do anything to warn those who are walking the wide road leading to destruction. True love is not mainly about being "nice". True love will do whatever is necessary to save a person's life, even if it is illegal, even if doing so has a high cost.

The real love of God is very, very powerful. If that love is actually in your heart, you will bear much fruit, and that fruit will endure. If the genuine love of God is in your heart, God will give you ways to express that love to those who need it most.

If the love of God isn't in your heart, it doesn't matter how sensitive, affirming, and tolerant you are. You won't accomplish anything. Your words will be lifeless and empty, and you actually have nothing to give a lost person.

Those who deviate from politically correct views on immigration will also be accused of being full of hate and fear. If you want the United States to enforce its immigration laws, the disciples of political correctness will accuse you of hating and fearing immigrants.

Hillary Clinton recently expressed her dream of an America without borders to a group of Brazilian investors. The fact that someone supports open borders does not mean that they love illegal immigrants or anyone else. You can follow all the rules of political correctness, but those rules will not change your heart. The rules of religion cannot change a man's heart, just as the rules of the Pharisees did not cause their hearts to be good.

I honor and respect the Hispanic people and culture. Some of most impressive, honorable, and loving people I have ever met are illegal Hispanic immigrants. I admire many of them and count it an honor to be friends with them. I would help them in any way that I could, and they have helped me many times. I would like to help them to find a legal way to stay in this country. They will become far better Americans than most Americans I know.

Nevertheless, I think that every nation should have clear laws on immigration and should enforce those laws. Quite simply, when a nation's legitimate representatives pass laws, those laws should be enforced. I think when a nation refuses to enforce its immigration laws, it creates a lawless situation, especially at the borders. Some of the most violent and depraved gangs in the entire world operate on the other side of our southern border, and America will pay a high price if we refuse to protect our borders.

The fact that someone believes that America should enforce its immigration laws does not mean that that person hates and fears immigrants! Many conservatives are simply tired of the lies that are told to them by politicians. They are tired of the lawlessness and chaos at our borders. They want to see immigration taking place in an orderly, law-abiding manner. They are tired of being condemned by liberals for desiring this.

THE NARROW-MINDEDNESS OF RELIGION

Those who are bound by religion have a very narrow-minded way of approaching every topic. Everything is viewed through the lens of their religion. For example, Jesus performed great miracles before the Pharisees. Instead of seeing the Son of God and the opportunity for salvation that stood before them, the Pharisees were busy analyzing everything through the lens of their religion. They were obsessed with finding some way that Jesus had broken their law so that they could accuse Jesus and continue living contentedly in their religious system. When Jesus performed miracles right in front of their eyes, the Pharisees were blind to the opportunity for faith that was before them. The only thing they could see was the fact that Jesus had performed His miracle on the Sabbath, breaking the system of rules they had created.

The followers of the Religion of Political Correctness do the same thing. They view every political and moral issue through the lens of their political correctness. If someone comes and speaks to them about the kingdom of heaven and performs miracles before them, they will react just like the Pharisees. They will search for some kind of prejudice, intolerance, or bias in the messenger. They will search for the ways that the messenger breaks their "laws" so that they can condemn him and ignore his message.

The social justice warriors of political correctness approach every issue in this way. The President can give a speech, dealing with current and real threats to America's security. The social justice warriors will ignore the real message of the speech, as they search for bias, prejudice, or intolerance in the words of the President.

This narrow-mindedness keeps people trapped in the bondage of their religion. They cannot really hear the message of the kingdom, because they are so busy analyzing the messenger to find the ways in which he breaks their rules.

THE SELF-RIGHTEOUS ANGER OF RELIGION

Perhaps the clearest indication that someone is bound by a religious spirit is found in their manifestation of self-righteous anger. People who are bound by religion are self-righteous and angry. This is true of the Pharisees, the Islamists, and the disciples of the Religion of Political Correctness.

The religious become absolutely enraged at those who break the rules of their religion, especially if the one breaking the rules is a true messenger of God. The Pharisees always tried to find some way that God's messengers had broken their law so that they could reject the message. The Pharisees put Stephen on trial for breaking the rules of their religion. During the trial, the face of Stephen shone like the face of an angel. As he spoke the Word of God to them, the Pharisees became so enraged that they began to gnash their teeth. Their hatred increased in intensity until they gathered stones and dragged Stephen away to stone him to death.

Likewise, the Pharisees brought Jesus Himself to trial before Pilate.

> **The High Priest asked Jesus, "Are you the Christ, the Son of the Blessed?" Jesus answered, "I am. And you will see the Son of Man sitting at the right hand of the Power, and coming with the clouds of heaven." Then the high priest tore his clothes and said, "What further need do we have of witnesses? You have heard the blasphemy! What do you think?" And they all condemned Him to be deserving of death (Mark 14:62-63).**

A deep, self-righteous anger burns in the heart of Islam. It burns toward those who refuse to follow the laws of Islam. It burns toward those who are chosen by God to be His vessels. It burns toward the Jews because of God's purposes for Israel. It burns toward true believers, who actually know God.

This is the rage that burns in the heart of every Islamic terrorist. The terrorist thinks that his rage comes from God. He believes that God is just as angry as he is at the people he desires to murder.

Religious anger usually pretends to be God's anger. The religious feel self-righteous in their anger because they are convinced that it is God's anger that they are feeling. In fact, it is the just the anger and bitterness of religion, the resentment of the cuckoo chick towards his brothers and sisters that think they have the right to share his nest.

The disciples of the Religion of Political Correctness can also be recognized by their anger. The disciples of political correctness hold loud, angry demonstrations when someone breaks their rules in even the most minor way. At Yale University, for example, the Intercultural Affairs Committee sent out a directive warning students not to wear Halloween costumes that could be interpreted as being culturally insensitive. One college professor, Erika Christakis, thought this heavy-handed advice was a bit too much. She sent out an email basically telling everyone to lighten up, to not be so super-sensitive, and to wear the Halloween costumes that they felt like wearing.

The social justice warriors of Yale University immediately jumped into action to avenge this blasphemous threat to the Religion of Political Correctness. A mob of hundreds of angry students surrounded the professor's husband as he tried to reason with them. These angry, intolerant students raged at the professor for her insensitivity and intolerance - shouting, screaming and shrieking. "You are disgusting!" they shrieked. "You should not sleep at night!"

The pressure became so intense that Erika ended up resigning from her faculty position. The administrators of Yale University refused to support her against the rage of the mob. They were unwilling to do anything that might offend the disciples of the Religion of Political Correctness.

The anger of the social justice warriors is both ridiculous and frightening. They now claim to be able to judge the prejudice that is in a person's heart by interpreting the "micro-aggressions" that the person commits. Using the new science of "micro-aggressions," the social justice warriors can find racism and intolerance in even the most innocuous of statements.

THE WORST OF MEN

Religious men believe that they are the best of men, because of how carefully they follow their own system of rules and regulations. In reality, they are often the worst of men. They use their religion as a cloak that covers up the darkness that is within. Jesus spoke about the religious Pharisees,

> **Woe to you, teachers of the law and Pharisees, you hypocrites! You clean the outside of the cup and dish, but inside they are full of greed and self-indulgence. Blind Pharisee! First clean the inside of the cup and dish, and then the outside also will be clean.**
>
> **Woe to you, teachers of the law and Pharisees, you hypocrites! You are like whitewashed tombs, which look beautiful on the outside but on the inside are full of the bones of the dead and everything unclean. In the same way, on the outside you appear to people as righteous but on the inside you are full of hypocrisy and wickedness** (Matthew 23:25-28).

Mohammed created a system of religious rules that made men appear holy on the outside, while the inside was deeply corrupt. Mohammed had many evil desires. When Mohammed desired his adopted son's wife, he received the revelation that God was giving the woman to him. When Mohammed wanted to take the property and women of his Jewish neighbors for himself, he received the revelation that God was giving him what he wanted. When Mohammed broke his promise to his wives and continued having sexual relations with Mary the slave girl, he received the revelation that he was allowed to break his promises. All of these revelations that allowed Mohammed to satisfy evil desires are written in the Koran and hadiths of Islam.

Mohammed and his followers performed their daily religious rituals as they raped and pillaged and murdered their way across the Arabian Peninsula. They seemed righteous and religious on the outside, but their hearts were filled with the same greed, selfish indulgence, hypocrisy, and lawlessness that filled the hearts of the Pharisees.

On America's campuses, the disciples of political correctness are extremely careful to follow the laws of their religion. They pride themselves in their righteousness, which in this religion is their tolerance and open-mindedness. Even as they obey the letter of their law, the same hypocrisy and self-indulgence that's found in all religions can be found in them. The disciples of political correctness are cruel and heartless toward anyone who breaks their rules, even as they pride themselves in their great cultural sensitivity. Despite bigotry and narrow-mindedness toward anyone who sees things differently from how they see them, they pride themselves on their tolerance. They engage in every form of sexual immorality as they pride themselves on their great openness to these sins. They call evil good, and good evil, as they accuse and condemn good men and drive them out of the universities. They live the easiest, most pampered existence imaginable, and yet they are skilled in convincing themselves that they are actually victims of oppression.

Jesus spoke a parable to the religious cuckoo birds of his day. Everyone who is bound by religion would do well to take His words to heart (Luke 18:9-11):

> **To some who were confident of their own righteousness and looked down on everyone else, Jesus told this parable: "Two men went up to the temple to pray, one a Pharisee and the other a tax collector. The Pharisee stood by himself and prayed: "God, I thank you that I am not like other people— robbers, evildoers, adulterers—or even like this tax collector. I fast twice a week and give a tenth of all I get."**
> **But the tax collector stood at a distance. He would not even look up to heaven, but beat his breast and said, "God, have mercy on me, a sinner."**
>
> **I tell you that this man, rather than the other, went home justified before God. For all those who exalt themselves will be humbled, and those who humble themselves will be exalted** (Luke 18:9-11).

6 CAIN AND ABEL

The stories of Eden were the backdrop of Cain's childhood. Mother and Father spoke of a different world, a different creation, a beautiful place, full of beauty and abundance. Cain saw the deep pain in Father's eyes as he told these stories.

CAIN'S OFFERING
Cain broke the surface of the hard ground with his stone-edged hoe. He scratched out two rows in the earth and deposited the seeds that he had gathered from the plants growing wild in the fields. It took him nearly the whole day to plant just three rows. At the end of the day, he looked upon the results of his labor with dissatisfaction.

Cain pondered his situation. This ground was cursed, and it would only grudgingly yield a harvest. Cain needed to spend most of his time laboring in the field just to provide enough harvest to survive. Was this really the way that he needed to spend his years? Did he really need to labor under the hot sun all the days of his life just to obtain food to eat? Surely there must be a better way. Somehow this curse must be broken. Perhaps he could give God a gift that would soften His heart toward him and his family.

An idea came into Cain's mind. He took ten large stones, and arranged them to form a crude altar with a fire pit in the middle. He arranged the wood and lit a fire with piece of flint he carried. Then he took some leftover grain from his last harvest, wrapped it in some large leaves, and laid the leaves and grain on the altar. The grain began to burn, and the smoke rose into the air.

Yet, even as the smoke of the grain rose into the heavens, Cain felt depressed. Somehow he knew that his offering wouldn't accomplish anything. How could it? The earth was cursed, and what came out of the earth was also cursed. Even his very body was cursed because it was made from the earth.

In discouragement, Cain walked away before the offering had even finished burning. He knew that it had been rejected and that the curse that was upon him and his family would continue.

A few days later, Cain was sitting at the edge of his field watching his brother Abel. Abel was singing a song to the Lord. There was joy on his face. His sheep were grazing around him.

Cain wondered what Abel's secret was. How could he be so joyful in such a situation? Didn't he understand that he and his family were cursed? Didn't he understand that the best they could hope for in life was to labor for their food until the day that they died? Even the animals had it better than Cain and his family. The animals didn't work for their food. They woke up in the morning and ate their fill from the grasses of the fields and the fruit of the trees. Only Cain had to work.

And there was Abel, singing with his sheep, worshiping God. Cain watched as Abel selected a healthy male sheep. He took the sheep to a stone altar that he had constructed. He laid his hands on the sheep's head and prayed. Cain could even hear the words that he prayed: "Oh Lord, my family and I have sinned. Please accept this lamb as a sacrifice. May the blood of this lamb cover our sins and remove them from your sight."

Cain watched as Abel slit the throat of the lamb. The lamb's blood spurted out, covering Abel's hands and arms. Then Abel laid the lamb upon the wood that he had gathered on the altar and lit the fire.

Cain watched the smoke ascending into the heavens, and he smelled the lamb roasting. After watching for a while, he moved away.

That night the family came together for dinner. Abel was beaming, almost unable to contain his joy. Cain was in a darker mood than usual, and Abel's joy irritated him.

After supper they sat down to discuss the day's events as their father desired. Abel poured out his words: "Father, I have been thinking about all that you told us, about the curse that was placed upon the land. As I was thinking and praying about these things, I fell asleep and received a dream. In the dream, I saw a lamb that had been slain. I heard a voice speaking in the dream, saying, 'Behold the Lamb of God, who takes away the sin of the world.' I didn't understand this dream, Father. How can a lamb take away sin?"

"But today, I did something very strange. I was singing songs to the Lord as I watched the sheep. Suddenly I felt an urge to give one of my best lambs as an offering to God. I chose the strongest, most perfect lamb in the flock. Then I killed it by cutting its throat. I took the body of the lamb and laid it on a fire that I built. I asked God to receive this lamb as an offering, a kind of payment for our sin."

Abel continued: "I'm not sure what happened, but as the smoke of the offering went into the sky, I felt a tremendous peace and joy filling my heart. I felt the presence of the Holy One. I felt His acceptance of the offering that I gave. I know that the lamb I offered is just a lamb. I know it's not the Lamb of God that I saw in my dream. Nevertheless, when I offered it to the Lord, I know that He accepted it. And if He accepted this offering, it must be possible for our sin to be forgiven by God and removed. If sin can be forgiven, the curse that is upon us can also be broken!"

Adam thought for a while, and then he spoke: "Cain and Abel, this story reminds me of what happened on the day that your mother and I sinned. After we ate from the tree that God forbade us to eat from, we felt so ashamed and afraid that we went and hid. The thought of facing the Lord absolutely terrified us. He had told us that on the day we eat of the tree, we would surely die. In our madness, we had eaten from that tree. We felt so guilty, so unworthy to stand before the Lord."

"Terror filled our hearts. Even our bodies seemed repulsive to us. We felt so ashamed and naked. We bound together some large leaves and made coverings for our bodies."

"When the Lord found us in our wretched state, He clothed us. He came to us as we hid. He took a sheep and killed it and skinned it. Then he took the skin and placed it upon our bodies. The skin of the sheep was still wet with blood, yet it comforted us and covered our nakedness."

"Somehow when the Lord killed the sheep and placed its skin upon us, I felt like he was speaking something to us through this action. That sheep was killed because of our sin. I feel like the life of that sheep was the only thing that kept us from being immediately destroyed when God found us hiding in shame."

Cain listened to the conversation. He watched Abel's shining face, and it irritated him. Why should Abel be favored in this way? Cain was the first one to think of giving God an offering, not Abel. Cain worked harder than Abel. Why should God accept Abel's offering of a sheep and reject the grain that he had worked so hard to produce?

The answer in Cain's mind was obvious. Abel was God's favorite. God loved Abel and forgave his sins. Cain had worked so hard to produce an offering that would please God, and yet God rejected him.

The next day Cain went back to his fields, and Abel went back to his sheep. Once again, Cain watched Abel from a distance. Abel wasn't working. He was singing and worshiping God as his sheep grazed. As Cain watched him, he felt bitter anger rising in his heart. Why was Abel so joyful and so favored by God? Cain almost felt like he could kill his brother.

Suddenly Cain was aware of a strong presence. He instinctively knew that it was the Presence of the Lord. The voice of the Lord came to Cain, "Why are you angry? And why has your countenance fallen? If you do well, will you not be accepted? And if you do not do well, sin lies at the door. And its desire is for you, but you should rule over it."

The Presence departed. Cain thought about the words he had received. He decided to ignore Abel and not to watch him any longer, lest he do something he would regret.

The following day, Cain was in the fields once again. The experience he had had the previous day with the Lord seemed almost unreal to him as he worked on the crops. The work filled his mind and thoughts. Once again he heard Abel's singing. He stood upright from his labor and watched him. A wave of resentment flooded over him as he watched Abel with his sheep.

Cain looked down at the heavy, stone–headed hoe that he used to break up the hard ground. He picked it up and began to walk toward his brother Abel.

As he approached Abel, Abel greeted him. "How are you, Brother? How are your crops doing?"

Cain exploded at Abel. "Are you mocking me? You know how they are doing. I work from early in the morning to late at night on in the fields, just so that you can have enough to eat! Meanwhile, you sit here singing with your sheep." Abel tried to calm Cain down saying, "Brother, someone needs to care for these sheep. You drink their milk and use the wool just as I do."

Cain wasn't listening. As Abel turned away, Cain suddenly swung his heavy stone-headed hoe with all of his strength. The hoe struck Abel on the back of his head, sinking into his skull with a sickening thud. Abel's body immediately collapsed to the ground in a heap, blood draining from his cracked skull into the soil.

Cain was shocked at what he had done. He dragged Abel's body into the bushes as he tried to decide what to do.

Finally Cain's heart calmed. He felt somehow satisfied that the issue was settled. What was done was done, and he might as well make the best of it. Abel was gone forever, and Cain could live his life without Abel's constant aggravation. Things might actually turn out to be better than they were before. Cain would never again have to compete with Abel for anything. He would no longer need to compete with Abel for his father's attention. Abel could no longer boast to him about his relationship with God. Nobody needed to know what had taken place.

Cain buried Abel's body. When he was finished, he sat down by the stream, washed his hands and prepared himself to face his father. As he sat there, the Presence from the previous day returned. Cain felt the words being spoken to him, "Cain, where is Abel your brother?"

Cain knew that he stood before God. He knew that this was the same God who had cursed the earth and condemned his parents to death because of disobedience. He knew that this was the God who loved his brother Abel and rejected him. Cain's response came out of his mouth in a hiss, "Am I my brother's keeper?"

The words were exhaled with a sharp, accusing force. Abel was God's favorite. Why didn't God look out for Abel if Abel were so special to him?

The Lord spoke again, "What have you done? The voice of your brother's blood cries out to Me from the ground. So now you are cursed from the earth, which has opened its mouth to receive your brother's blood from your hand. When you till the ground it shall no longer yield its strength to you. A fugitive and a vagabond you shall be on the earth."

The words hit Cain like a like a hammer, breaking him down. Cain had strived for years to please his father and to please God. After all his striving, he was being rejected by the Lord and cast away from his home and family.

Feelings of rejection and hopelessness overwhelmed Cain. He cried out, "My punishment is greater than I can bear! Surely You have driven me out this day from the face of the ground; I shall be hidden from Your face; I shall be a fugitive and a vagabond on the earth, and it will happen that anyone who finds me will kill me."

At that moment, the only thing Cain could feel was his rejection. Everything seemed so unfair. All his life he had struggled with the curse upon the ground and the curse that had come upon his family. He had tried to bring God an offering that could lift the curse. And now an even greater curse was being placed upon him. He was being cast out of his home, cast out of his farm, cast out of his profession. No longer could he be a tiller of the earth. The earth, which had grudgingly given him a living, was turning against him. God Himself was rejecting him.

As feelings of bitterness and rejection overflowed out of Cain's heart, the voice of the Lord came again,

"Therefore, whoever kills Cain, vengeance shall be taken on him sevenfold."

This became Cain's solace and comfort in the days ahead. He was rejected by God. He was cast out from his home and family. His only comfort was found in bitterness and revenge against anyone who crossed him. Whoever harmed him would be harmed seven times worse than he was.

CAIN AND RELIGION

The story of Cain and Abel is the story of the struggle between the sons of God and the sons of religion. Cain was a religious man, and Abel represents the sons of God. The religious man strives under a curse, for whoever is under the law is under a curse. The religious man strives to create an offering that will please God.

This religious offering is always rejected by God. A religious offering, offered by the religious mind of man according to the ways of man, can never please God. Cain's offering was not acceptable to God. It was a cursed offering, coming from a cursed earth.

There was only one offering that was acceptable to God. The only acceptable offering was the blood of the Perfect Lamb. Somehow, Abel received revelation about the Lamb of God. Somehow, he knew that the offering that was acceptable in the sight of God came from the blood of a perfect lamb. Somehow, Abel was able to look prophetically at the Christ who was to come. As he offered the firstborn lamb of his flock to the Lord, he looked forward to the Lamb of God, the firstborn Son of God, whose life was given for the sins of the world.

We do the same thing when we drink the wine of Communion. We remember the blood of Jesus Christ that was shed for our sins. We put our trust in the blood covenant that we have with God through the blood of Jesus Christ. We look back to what took place at the cross. Abel looked forward to what would happen at the cross.

God respected Abel and His offering. Abel was walking on the path of reconciliation with God. When Abel received the revelation that the only acceptable offering before God was the blood of a firstborn male lamb, he was being led by the Spirit of God. The Bible teaches us: **"For as many as are led by the Spirit of God, these are sons of God."** (Romans 8:14)

The Bible says that the testimony of Jesus is the spirit of prophecy (Rev. 19:10). As the Spirit of God led Abel, he received prophetic revelation regarding Jesus Christ, the perfect, acceptable sacrifice, the perfect Lamb of God, who takes away the sin of the world.

Cain didn't understand the offering that God wanted. Cain heard the voice of God, but he didn't really know God. With his religious mind, he formulated an offering that he thought would please God. He worked to produce this offering by the sweat of his brow.

You might say that Cain created his own form of religion, his own way of coming to God. Unfortunately, the striving of religious men never actually brings them to God. Men put their faith in their own religious deeds, their own works, and their own offerings, thinking that these will be pleasing to God. A Muslim hopes that his prayer and good deeds will make him righteous in the sight of God and pay for his sins. The Pharisee puts his trust in his own system of laws and his own obedience to those laws, hoping that his obedience to the law will justify him in the sight of God.

CAIN AND BABEL
The religious strivings of Cain can also be seen in his spiritual descendants, the builders of the Tower of Babel. In the days following

the Great Flood, the offspring of Noah did not want to be scattered across the face of the earth. They wanted to build a great city with a tower that would rise into the heavens.

The Tower of Babel was actually a temple built of bricks. This brick temple represents man-made religions. Bricks made of mud and clay represent human labor and striving, and brick temples represent man's effort to save himself. But man cannot save himself, no matter how hard he works. He needs a Savior.

The Tower of Babel was a place where men hoped to connect with God. In reality, the temples built by bricks never connect men with the true God. Temples made with bricks can only connect men to false gods, fallen angels that live in rebellion to the true God. These false gods unite with fallen men to build religions that blaspheme the true God. The Tower of Babel would surely have become a place where blood sacrifices would have been offered and blood covenants would have been made with the fallen angels of the Evil One.

ARAB IDOLATRY

Many years ago the Arabs of Mecca had a shrine where they kept their idols known as the Kaaba. The Kaaba was home to 360 idols. Built into the eastern corner of the Kaaba was a black stone that was highly revered by the Arabs. The Arabs worshiped idols and stones during those days (Bukhari 6:661). They performed animal sacrifices as they worshiped their stones, idols, and evil spirits at the Kaaba. They smeared the blood of sacrificed animals on the stones, forming blood covenants with the evil spirits represented by the stones.

Before worshiping their stones and idols, the Arabs would enter a state known as Ihram. They would perform ritual washings to cleanse themselves before their acts of worship. Sometimes they would wear special garments as a part of the worship (Bukhari 2:703).

During their ceremonies of idol worship, the Arabs marched around the Kaaba and kissed the black stone as they passed it. They also marched around two hills known as As-Safa and Al-Marwah. As they marched, they called out the names of their false gods. One of those gods was Hubal, the moon god. His symbol was the crescent moon.

The tribe responsible for the pagan rituals of the Kaaba was the Quraysh. One day a prophet, Mohammed, arose from the tribe of Quraysh, claiming to be sent from God. He called the Arabs to turn away from their idolatry to worship the true God. This prophet began a new religion that focused on the worship of one God and the destruction of all idolatry.

This prophet disposed of the 360 small idols that were set up in and around the Kaaba and began his new religion. He kept the big idol, the Kaaba itself, and the black stone. He also kept the rituals of idol worship as he formed his new religion.

Mohammed taught his followers to march around the Kaaba as they followed his new religion, just as their ancestors had. He taught them to point to the black stone and call out the name of their god as they passed it. He taught them to kiss the black stone, just as their pagan ancestors did. He taught them to bow down to the Kaaba, the house of idols, five times a day for prayer. He taught his followers to march in circles around As-Safa and Al-Marwah just as their pagan ancestors did. He commanded his followers to go on pilgrimage at least once in their lifetime to the Kaaba, to worship there just as their ancestors did. He taught his followers about the special clothes they should wear on pilgrimage, the special way to wash themselves, and the state of Ihram. He taught them to perform blood sacrifices at the Kaaba as part of their pilgrimage.

Today hundreds of millions of Moslems are following the idolatrous rituals of Islam, rituals that come straight from the idol worship of pagan Arab tribes. The evidence that these rituals all come straight from Arab paganism does not come from Islam's enemies. The evidence is found in the Islamic scriptures themselves. These rituals bind them in covenants with the same spirits that bound the pagan Arabs of times past. The symbol of Islam is the crescent moon, the symbol of the false God Hubal.

The religions of Cain and the religions of Babel cause men to march in endless circles, just as Muslims march around the Kaaba today. Every religion formed by men is like a miniature Tower of Babel that pretends to offer a doorway into heaven. These doorways never lead to God but instead to the bondage and the rebellion of the Evil One. As men strive to come to God through these doorways, they always end up in deeper bondage to their religion and their gods.

The reality of life without a Savior is horrifying. There is only sin and bondage and the broad path leading to destruction. The religions of Babel hide this fundamental reality. These religions offer substitutes that help to blind people's eyes and deaden their hearts so that they do not see the horror of their lost condition. The religions of Babel seem to offer hope and a path to immortality. The brick temples of Babel seem to offer a path by which people can climb out of their miserable existence. Each religion offers something that seems more attractive than the reality of eternal judgment.

Only Christianity exposes mankind's truly lost and hopeless state. Christianity exposes our desperate need for a Savior. There is no hope apart from God. There is no salvation apart from God. There is no goodness apart from God. **"All we like sheep have gone astray; We have turned, every one, to his own way; And the Lord has laid on Him the iniquity of us all"** (Isaiah 53:6).

The altar and the temple of the living God are not made out of bricks. They are made out of stones. The temple of the Lord during the last days will be made out of living stones (I Peter 2:5). These stones are the lives that have been transformed by the power of God. This temple cannot be built through human striving. It can only be built by the power of God as people give themselves fully unto Him.

BITTERNESS AND REJECTION IN RELIGION

There is a deep bitterness and rejection in religion. The sons of religion pay a high price as they prepare their offerings for God, but their offerings are not accepted by God. The sons of religion carry heavy burdens, hard to bear, and nobody helps them to carry them (Matthew 23:4). They strive to please God, but their efforts are in vain.

The religious man feels superior in his heart of hearts. Cain felt resentful toward Abel because he was sure that he deserved God's favor more than Abel. He was the firstborn. He worked harder than Abel. If God were fair, He would have favored Cain over his brother. If God were fair, He would have accepted Cain's offering. There was only one conceivable explanation in Cain's mind. God wasn't fair. Cain worked so long and so hard, and yet God had rejected him.

Cain never realized that in fact he was the cuckoo chick, the son of religion whose heart was set against both God and his brother. If Cain had been teachable, he would have learned from his brother's example. He would have learned something about the kind of offering God was looking for.

If Cain had been teachable, he would have taken to heart the warning that God gave him. God himself confronted Cain in his jealousy before he killed his brother and asked him, "Why are you angry? And why has your countenance fallen? If you do well, will you not be accepted?" Religion always manifests with self-righteous anger. Cain's anger was the anger of the Pharisees, the anger of an Islamic extremist.

Religious men are stubborn. They are not teachable. They are convinced that they understand the righteousness of God. They are convinced that they have achieved a righteousness that is greater than those around them. They believe that God should honor their righteousness and favor them over others. They would rather judge God, and consider Him unfair, than to truly humble themselves and receive correction.

Men hold on to their religion even when it obviously isn't working, even when God Himself rebukes them. I have seen religious men warned in supernatural ways who still refuse to budge on their religious opinions. They refuse to repent. They refuse to put aside their religious justifications for their actions. They continue to cloak themselves with religious explanations and excuses for the things that they do.

Most of all, they refuse to put their religion aside to be taught by the Lord. They are so convinced they know the answers, that they become deaf and blind, with hardened hearts. Nothing gets through their religious defenses. They refuse to take the words of Jesus to heart: **"Except you become as little children, you cannot enter the kingdom of heaven"** (Matthew 18:3).

Even after Cain had murdered his brother and had been confronted by God with his sin, he refused to repent. Cain knew that the price of sin was death. He knew what he had done to his brother. Nevertheless, when God had mercy on Cain and instead of killing him, had him cast out as a fugitive, Cain responded with a bitter cry: "My punishment is greater than I can bear! Surely You have driven me out this day from the face of the ground; I shall be hidden from Your face; I shall be a fugitive and a vagabond on the earth, and it will happen that anyone who finds me will kill me."

THE SPIRIT OF MURDER
Cain had to be cast out of his family. Cain was the cuckoo chick. He hated his brother, a son of God who was led by the Spirit of God. Eve would soon have another son, Seth who would replace Abel. Eve said of Seth, "God has appointed another seed for me instead of Abel, whom Cain killed." Seth became the father of the righteous, the father of those who called upon the Lord, the father of Enoch and Noah and every other son of God.

If Cain had not been driven out of the family, what would have happened next? Because Cain never repented of his jealousy and hatred, if Cain had been allowed to remain, that same jealousy and anger would have turned against Seth, Abel's replacement. Cain would surely have murdered Seth. That's what cuckoo chicks do.

There is a struggle between the sons of God and the sons of religion. The sons of religion desire to displace the sons of God. They desire to throw them out of the nest and take their place. If they are not removed, they will murder the sons of God.

7 ISHMAEL AND ISAAC

ISHMAEL

Ishmael grew up as the favored son, the firstborn son, the only son of his father. His father was a wealthy man, a tribal leader who led his flocks and his people through the grazing lands of Canaan. Ishmael held a special place in the community, a place that none of the other young men could challenge. He was the son who would fulfill the promises that God gave to Abraham.

Ishmael's father was no ordinary man. Ishmael's father was Abraham. Abraham was a man who met with God and talked with God. God gave Abraham amazing promises. He promised to bless Abraham and make him a blessing. He promised that Abraham's descendants would be like the sand of the seashore, and that he would be the father of many nations.

For 25 years, Abraham and his family wandered through the lands of Canaan. Abraham's flocks multiplied, and his community prospered. Eventually Abraham's men composed a small army of more than 300 men and the community reached nearly 1000 people.

Ishmael's mother was Hagar, the servant woman of Abraham's wife Sarah. For as long as Ishmael could remember, Hagar and Sarah clashed with one another. Even as Hagar obeyed Sarah's every command, she seethed with resentment against her. When she and Ishmael were alone, we can easily envision that she told her son the reasons she despised Sarah so much. Her story probably went like this:

Ishmael, I served Sarah faithfully for many years. Sarah was my mistress, and I always obeyed her, even when it was difficult. Sarah wasn't a very happy woman. She always wanted to give her husband a son, but she couldn't. This fact upset her greatly, and she often seemed discouraged. One day she came to me with a plan that she had come up with. She said to me, "Hagar, you know that Abraham and I need to have a son. It is the only way that God's great promises can be fulfilled. I am simply too old to have a child myself. I have decided to give you to my husband for a time, so that you can have a son in my name. You are my servant, and if you have a child with my husband, the child will be mine."

Sarah didn't ask me my opinion about her plan. She just told me what was going to happen. The next night Abraham arrived at my door, and we spent the night together. I soon realized that I had become pregnant. I knew that when you were born, Sarah would claim you as her own. I knew one thing – the child inside me belonged to me and Abraham, not to Sarah.

For the first time in my life, I began to stand up to Sarah. It wasn't my fault that she wasn't able to have a child. I was the one who God allowed to become pregnant with the child who would fulfill his promise to give Abraham many descendants, not Sarah. And so for the first time, I began to speak my mind to Sarah. When she tried to boss me around, I refused to obey her. When she ordered me to fetch water for her, I refused and told her to fetch it herself.

I didn't realize that Sarah would turn Abraham against me. She went to Abraham and told him a lot of lies about me. She told Abraham that I was a very rebellious servant, even though I served her faithfully many years. Abraham listened to her lies and gave her permission to do what she wanted with me.

From that moment on, my life became miserable. Sarah went out of her way to mistreat me. Even as my pregnancy progressed, Sarah ordered me to do difficult jobs, cursed me, and even struck me. Finally I decided to run away. I ran into the wilderness, to a place where I knew I could find some water. There I sat by that spring, desperate, afraid, and alone.

Suddenly a man appeared. He seemed to come from nowhere. He was a very unusual man. He seemed to have great authority. He asked me what I was doing in that place. I told him: "I am fleeing from the presence of my mistress Sarai."

He spoke to me and told me to return to my mistress and serve her. He told me that God had heard my cries. He told me that when you were born I should name you Ishmael and that you would have many descendants.

When he said that to me, I knew that God had chosen me over Sarah. I knew that you would be the one whom God would use to fulfill the promises he gave to our master Abraham. And so I returned home. It didn't matter to me what Sarah might do to me. I knew that God had spoken to me and that Sarah could not take my son. I knew that we would rise, and Sarah would fall. I know that God will cause you to have many descendants and make you into a great nation.

Reading the lines and between the lines of Genesis 16-18, we can gain understanding of Ishmael's development from childhood to manhood. As Ishmael listened to his mother's words, he surely felt her pain from the past and her faith in him. He vowed in his heart that he would make his mother proud, that he would walk out the promises that God had given to his father and mother.

Ishmael loved his father and felt a special connection with him. He knew his father loved him and valued him highly. He saw the hope and pride in his father's eyes when he looked at him. He knew that his father saw God's promises being fulfilled through his son. Abraham had been given so many promises by God. Ishmael felt proud to be Abraham's son, proud to be chosen by God to fulfill such promises.

Ishmael shared his mother's resentment against Sarah. He never allowed Sarah to treat him as her son. When she tried to pull him close, he always pushed her away. He only spoke to her when he needed to. When his father was listening, he spoke to Sarah with a strained politeness. When his father wasn't around, he made a show of ignoring Sarah completely. Usually, he simply had nothing to do with her. In his heart, he thought that Sarah must have done something very bad to be cursed with barrenness,

As time went on, the hope of the community centered upon Ishmael. He was obviously the fulfillment of the prophecies given to Abraham. Sarah was in her eighties, long past the years of childbearing; and Abraham himself was 100 years old. Ishmael was Abraham's only son. The whole community knew the promises that had been given to Abraham and the promises that were given to Hagar in the wilderness. They put two and two together and began to celebrate Ishmael as the son of promise. Ishmael would surely become the father of many nations and fulfill the promises given to Abraham.

And so Ishmael grew as a kind of prince in the community, the apple of his father's eye. The adults favored Ishmael. Ishmael lorded it over the other boys his age, who were intimidated by him. Even when disputes and fights broke out with the other boys, they feared to stand up to him. They feared what Abraham would do if anything happened to him. Ishmael's confidence and arrogance grew.

ISHMAEL'S WORLD IN CRISIS

Then it happened, the day that Ishmael's world fell apart. Early in the morning, Abraham had an encounter with the Lord. The words that the Lord spoke affected everybody. But for Ishmael, they were devastating.

Abraham gathered the entire community and said to them:

"This morning, I met the Lord. He spoke to me again about the great promises that He would fulfill through me. My descendants will fill the earth. I will be the father of many nations, and the land of Canaan will be given to us as an inheritance."

Abraham continued, "This time, the Lord spoke to me that we must enter a covenant with him. In this covenant, He becomes our God, and we become his people. The sign of this covenant is circumcision. Every male must be circumcised. This is a holy ceremony, a joining of ourselves to the Lord."

And so the circumcisions began. Abraham's word was law in this community. Ishmael took his turn with the others. Abraham himself performed the circumcisions with the help of the blacksmith. When Ishmael's turn came, the pain was intense, but Ishmael was proud and strong and didn't flinch.

After the circumcisions were completed, there was a camaraderie among the young men and in the community as a whole. They had all passed through quite a trial, and it bonded them with one another as well as to the Lord. No longer was it just Abraham who had a connection with God. Now they were all the children of God, united in covenant with the God of Abraham.

It was in the evening that Ishmael felt things falling apart. He was sitting outside his father's tent, when he heard his father inside talking with Sarah. "Sarah," Abraham said, "the Lord spoke something else to me today. He told me that you would become pregnant and have a son. When He spoke it to me, I laughed. It seemed so ridiculous to me. And yet, it will take place. The word of the Lord will be fulfilled. You will have a son, and he will be the son of promise who will fulfill God's promises to us."

Ishmael's heart turned to ice as the words penetrated his heart. Suddenly, his world turned upside down. Everything he believed in suddenly seemed to be falling apart. Wasn't he the one who would fulfill the prophecies? Wasn't he the one chosen by His father and by the Lord? How was it possible that Sarah could have a son at such an age, a son who would fulfill the promises given to Abraham? He remembered the story of how Sarah and Abraham had rejected his mother when she was pregnant and how she fled to the wilderness. He felt like the same rejection was returning. Confusion and anger crept into his thoughts.

Several months passed. Abraham and Sarah spent much of their time together. One day, a visitor met with Abraham under a tree. When the visitor left, people started talking about the visit, saying that the visitor was a messenger from the Lord, or perhaps the Lord Himself.

Sarah seemed thrilled by the visit. Evidently, she had listened to the conversation from inside the tent. Something that had been said thrilled her. She bubbled with excitement and laughter, telling everyone she met, "I am going to have a son! She seemed so confident of this that it was difficult for people to doubt her. Her certainty and her joy were so infectious that those around her accepted her words. The happier Sarah became, the more depressed Ishmael felt.

Time passed. A messenger arrived from far away. He brought the news that Sodom and Gomorrah had been destroyed by fire. This was shocking news. Everyone knew how evil Sodom was. Now it no longer existed. Abraham told the community that God had told him that Sodom was to be destroyed because of its great sin.

At the same time, it became clear that another prophecy had been fulfilled. Sarah was pregnant, at ninety years of age. Sarah was so joyful. She went everywhere telling the story of what had happened. She told people how God had come to them and had told them that she would have a child. She told them that this son would be the promised son, the son who would carry the covenant of God and the blessing of God into the nations.

Hagar and Ishmael felt their place of honor in the community slipping away. The gang of young men who followed Ishmael around began to splinter. Fights broke out between the young men. Ishmael himself was challenged several times to fight by young men who never would have challenged him in the past.

When Isaac was born, the community came together in joy--except for Ishmael and Hagar--who stood at a distance watching the celebration. Ishmael cursed the child in his heart. He saw the child as the representative of everything that was wrong in the world. He hated Sarah, who had cast him and his mother into the wilderness, who had struggled with his mother so many times. He hated the new baby. He hated the look on Sarah's face as she gazed at him.

On the day that Isaac was weaned, the community held a celebration. Everyone was joyful. Abraham spoke publicly about the promises of God that he had received.

Ishmael stood at the edge of the crowd, seething with resentment. He spoke to some of the young men who were nearby, "That's the ugliest baby I've ever seen. Something is wrong with him. I think he might have some problems in his head."

Sarah overheard Ishmael's comments. She didn't say anything at the time, but she immediately walked away and looked for Abraham. She pulled him aside, and spoke so loudly that people could hear: "Cast out the servant woman and her son! My son cannot share the inheritance with Ishmael!" Abraham didn't say anything.

The next day, Abraham came in a different way. He called Hagar and Ishmael together and said to them, "The Lord met with me this morning and told me that you need to leave. I cannot have division in this community. A house divided cannot stand." Then he looked directly into Ishmael's eyes and said, "Son, don't be afraid. God will take care of you, and make you a great nation."

With those final words, Abraham gave Hagar a supply of bread and a goatskin filled with water, and Ishmael and Hagar walked out of the community into the wilderness to begin their new life.

ISHMAEL RELIGION

Not every religion is started by evil men with evil intentions. Not every religion begins with demonic revelations. Not every religion begins in the cave of Hira where Mohammed received his first revelations. An "angel" grabbed Mohammed and forced him to recite the words of the Koran. Mohammed was actually convinced that he was possessed by an evil spirit until his wife Khadijah convinced him that his revelations came from God.

Unlike Islam, there are many religions and religious systems that originate in the minds and hearts of good men who know God, love God, and desire to serve Him. Although they love God, these men are not led by the Holy Spirit as they work for God. They form religious systems according to their own human reasoning. They are led by the flesh and not the spirit.

These men form Ishmael ministries. The product of our own thinking that is well intentioned but not directed by the Spirit of God will always produce an Ishmael. God can use Ishmael to a certain degree, but Ishmael cannot fulfill God's purposes for a nation.

Isaac ministries are very different from Ishmael ministries. An Isaac ministry is a ministry through which the Lord fulfills his good promises. An Isaac ministry does not depend on the wisdom of man, the timing of man, or the resources of man. An Isaac ministry draws from the resources of the kingdom of heaven and brings the kingdom of heaven to the earth.

Sarah and Abraham made a plan to fulfill God's promise using Sarah's maid Hagar. Abraham and Sarah knew God and loved him. They had encounters with God and received promises from him. Yet Sarah and Abraham were human, and in the case of Hagar they walked in the presumption of their flesh instead of in faith and obedience to the Spirit of God.

The bodies of Abraham and Sarah were old. Sarah did not think it was possible for God to give her a son at such an old age. So she made a different plan in order to help God out a bit. She gave her maidservant Hagar to Abraham as his concubine. She said, **"See now, the Lord has restrained me from bearing children. Please, go in to my maid; perhaps I shall obtain children by her."** (Genesis 16:2) In this way, Hagar conceived and gave birth to a son, Ishmael.

Sarah believed the promises of God, but she thought that God would use a logical way to fulfill His promises. She speculated and decided, "Perhaps I just need to make my own plans, and trust that God will bless my plans." The only plan she could think of was to send her maid Hagar to Abraham so that Hagar could have a son that could be claimed by Abraham and Sarah.

In reality, the only way that God's promise could actually be fulfilled was through a true miracle. There was no earthly way for Abraham and Sarah to fulfill God's promise. It didn't matter how hard they tried or how much they prayed. A miracle needed to take place for God's plans to be fulfilled.

For a time, it seemed like Sarah's plans were working. Sarah sent Hagar to her husband, and Hagar became pregnant with a son. Everyone rejoiced. But even as it seemed that Sarah's plans were succeeding, something rose up in Hagar's heart against Sarah. Hagar began to despise Sarah, probably because Sarah assumed that Hagar's son would belong to her. And so even as Ishmael was developing in Hagar's womb, strife and division came to the household of Abraham. Strife and division always accompany the works of the flesh. Strife and division always accompany Ishmael ministries.

In Galatians, Paul writes that Ishmael was born to a bondwoman (slave) according to the flesh, while Isaac was born to a freewoman through promise. Ishmael represents a work of the flesh, a product of human reasoning and motivations. Paul describes some of the characteristics of the works of the flesh in the following chapter. They include hatred, contentions, jealousies, outbursts of wrath, selfish ambitions, dissensions, heresies, envy, murders. Division and strife followed Ishmael all the days of his life. Every man's hand was against him, and his hand was against every man (Genesis 16:12).

Ishmael was blessed by God, who promised Ishmael that he would have many descendants. Ishmael was circumcised, as were all of Abraham's servants. This circumcision was the sign that Ishmael was a part of the covenant that Abraham had with God. Ishmael was loved by his father Abraham, who hoped that God could use Ishmael to fulfill the promises that God had given Abraham. Nevertheless, Ishmael was the son born according to the flesh, not according to the Spirit.

Ishmael ministries can be blessed by God and used to a certain degree by God. These ministries have a covenant with God. The persons involved have received salvation as they put their trust in Jesus. Nevertheless, Ishmael ministries are not led by the Holy Spirit. Even though they have a covenant with God, they do not walk closely with

God in that covenant. They prefer to do things their own way, in their own timing. God is able to bless these ministries to a certain degree, in a certain season, but in the end such ministries are not able to fulfill His promises on the earth. God allows these Ishmael ministries to remain until Isaac is born.

Just as Abraham and Sarah walked in great presumption as they assumed they could use their own methods to bring about the fulfillment of God's promise, Ishmael ministries walk in presumption. They think they know what God wants to do without asking the Lord. They know that they have a covenant with God and that He will bless the work of their hands. They know that God wants the world to hear the gospel. But they do not think it is necessary to walk closely to the Lord and to know His voice. They make major decisions based on human judgment instead of seeking the mind of the Lord.

Ishmael ministries don't see the importance of doing things in God's timing. For an Ishmael ministry, any time is a good time. It is not necessary to wait on the Lord. God's blessing was on Ishmael, and Ishmael took part in Abraham's covenant with God. Likewise, many Ishmael ministries do not understand the value of waiting for God's instructions or waiting for God's timing. Why should they wait? God has already promised to bless them. They are part of a covenant with God. They already know what to do, so why not just do it?

In this way, Ishmael ministries make their plans and push forward and do them. They are confident in God's blessing and in their own abilities. They have the knowledge and the resources to succeed. And for a while, they do succeed. God blesses their work, and it grows and prospers.

For a while, Ishmael seemed to be more successful than Isaac. Ishmael grew to be a strong young man, while Isaac was just a baby. In the same way, Ishmael ministries often seem to be running ahead of other ministries. Ishmael leaders read the latest books and implement the latest church-growth. strategies. They have the best websites and quality materials. They think they are on the cutting edge of what God is doing in their nation.

But Ishmael ministries have not needed to overcome death. They have not needed to overcome impossible circumstances. Therefore, when death and impossible circumstances come upon a nation, an Ishmael ministry has no answers. An Ishmael ministry can succeed quite well in a time of prosperity. An Ishmael ministry can even seem to be an Isaac ministry that is fulfilling God's purposes in a land. But when the time of testing comes, an Ishmael ministry is exposed for what it is. It is a ministry of the flesh, not of the Spirit. It is a human organization that functions by human principles. It is not the kingdom of heaven.

No matter how hard Ishmael strives, there is a limitation upon Ishmael. Ishmael ministries may be blessed by God, but they will always miss out on the highest purposes of God. When it comes time for God's highest purposes to be fulfilled, Isaac must be born. Only Isaac, the son of promise, can fulfill God's promises for a nation.

ISAAC REPRESENTS RESURRECTION LIFE

When God spoke to Abraham and Sarah that Sarah would give birth to a son in her old age, they realized that a miracle needed to take place. They realized that God's promises could only be accomplished with supernatural power. Sarah was old, and her womb was dead, and Abraham was more than one hundred years old.

But Abraham and Sarah did not look at their dying bodies or their failing strength. Instead, their faith was strengthened. They believed God. They were fully convinced that God was able to do what He had promised. And so at the time set by God, Isaac was born. His birth was a miracle. Romans 4:19 says that Abraham's body was already dead and Sarah's womb was dead. Isaac's birth was nothing less than a demonstration of resurrection power.

Likewise, there are ministries being birthed in extraordinary conditions. In some of the most spiritually oppressed countries on earth, there are men and woman who have fully believed the promises of God for their nation. They do not look at the feeble, dead state of the church in their nation. They look at the promise of God, and they hold onto the promise of God. These are the Isaac ministries.

Isaac ministries are started in impossible circumstances that would cause any rational person to give up. Isaac ministries are not usually started by people with a lot of resources and training. They are started by people who have nothing to hold on to but the Lord and His promises. They cannot rely on natural wisdom or natural strength because they simply don't have very much of either.

Because Isaac ministries are birthed in impossible circumstances, as they grow up, they will not be bound by circumstances. Isaac ministries truly have the potential to transform nations. When everything appears dark, an Isaac ministry will continue to hold on to the promises of God for that nation. When warfare spreads destruction in a nation, an Isaac ministry will continue to believe God's good promises and to take action.

When famine came to the land of Canaan before Isaac was born, Abraham took his family and moved to Egypt. It didn't seem possible for him to stay in Canaan during the famine. But when a second famine afflicted the land of Canaan during the days when Isaac was the community leader, God spoke to Isaac and told him to remain in Canaan. And so Isaac remained and planted his crops in a time of famine. Instead of starving, he reaped a hundredfold return (Genesis 26:12). Isaac was born in impossible conditions, and he is able to prosper and be fruitful in impossible conditions.

The prophet Daniel talks of a time of great trouble that will come upon the earth, a time of trouble that is worse than the world has ever seen. (Daniel 12:1) But in the same passage, he says that **"Those who are wise shall shine like the brightness of the firmament, And those who turn many to righteousness like the stars forever" (12:3).** These are the people of the Isaac ministries that will walk in the wisdom of God and turn many to righteousness. They will do this even in the great darkness of the end times. Stars shine the brightest at nighttime, and these saints will shine brightest when circumstances appear to be the worst.

THE TIMING OF GOD

Those who seek the instructions of the Lord must be willing to wait on the Lord to actually speak to them. God's timing is usually very different from man's time. God's time for Isaac to be born seemed to be fifty years too late. But Isaac can only be brought to birth in the timing of the Lord.

An Isaac ministry can only be birthed in God's timing. An Ishmael ministry can be birthed in man's timing. An Isaac ministry must wait on the Lord. An Isaac ministry must understand God's timing in a nation. There is a time to sow and a time to reap. There is a time of growth and a time of rest. An Isaac ministry does the right thing at the right time.

They that wait on the Lord shall renew their strength. They shall mount up with wings as eagles. They shall run and not be weary, they shall run and not faint. (Isaiah 40:31)

To wait on the Lord does not mean that you sit around watching television as you passively wait for the Lord to show up. To wait on the Lord means that you work wholeheartedly to do what God wants you to do in the season that you are in. It means doing the right thing at the right time. When it is time to prepare yourself for ministry, you prepare yourself by going deeper in the Word and deeper in intercession. When it is time to cry out to God for your nation, you cry out to Him, spending nights in prayer and intercession. When it is time to preach, you preach the gospel with power, with everything that is in you. As you walk closely to the Lord, hearing and obeying His instructions and doing the right thing at the right time, you will find that supernatural grace is released upon your life to succeed.

King Saul is an example of an Ishmael-type ministry in the Bible. King Saul won many battles, but he did not walk closely to the Lord or inquire of the Lord's instructions. God could use King Saul to a certain degree, but the high purposes of God could only be fulfilled by David.

In contrast, David regularly sought the instructions of the Lord. David spent much of his life fighting the Philistines. He was an expert on fighting the Philistines. But when David was faced with battle, he did not presume to know what he should do. He didn't make major decisions based on his great experience. He always stopped and inquired of the Lord. In one battle he was told to go out immediately and fight and the Philistines would be delivered into his hand (II Samuel 5: 19). In another battle the Lord told David to circle around behind the enemy and not to attack until he heard the sound of marching in the tops of the mulberry trees. This was the sign that the Lord's army was marching out ahead of David to fight the battle for David (II Samuel 5: 23-25). In a similar way, an Isaac ministry must be willing to seek the Lord's instructions. The Lord's ways are not our ways. His ways are higher than our ways. His thoughts are higher than our thoughts. (Isaiah 55:9) We need to hear from Him. We need to walk in wisdom.

ISAAC BELONGS TO THE LORD

Isaac represents resurrection power. Isaac was formed in the "dead" womb of his mother. His birth represented life from the dead. Later on in Isaac's life, we see the symbols of resurrection once again. God put a test before Abraham. He asked Abraham to offer his son as a burnt offering on Mount Moriah. Amazingly enough, Abraham obeyed. As he raised his knife to kill his son, the angel of the Lord called to him from heaven:

> **"Abraham, Abraham!... Do not lay your hand on the lad, or do anything to him, for now I know that you fear God, since you have not withheld your son, your only son from me." Then Abraham lifted up his eyes and saw a ram caught with his horns in a thicket. Abraham took the ram, and offered it as a burnt offering before the Lord in the place of his son. (Genesis 22:1-14)**

The amazing thing about this story is that Abraham did these things in faith. The Bible says that Abraham concluded that "God was able to raise (Isaac) up, even from the dead" (Hebrews 11:19). Abraham had seen Isaac born in an impossible situation, and he believed that God would surely raise Isaac from the dead even if he was sacrificed. Isaac is a symbol of resurrection life.

Isaac represents those who walk closely with the Lord, those who take up their cross and follow Jesus. Abraham walked in such unity with God, that when God asked him to lay Isaac on the altar, he obeyed. This level of trusting obedience is almost unimaginable today. Abraham was literally willing to sacrifice his son, believing that God would raise him up again.

Isaac also represents the amazing steps of faith that the sons of God are willing to take. Just as Abraham believed God's word and took an action of incredible faith and risk, Isaac ministries are willing to take incredible steps of faith as they obey the Lord. Isaac ministries are willing to go places where Ishmael would not dare to enter. They are willing to risk everything to obey the Lord when the Lord speaks to them. They believe in the God of the Resurrection, and they move in resurrection power.

THE FINAL HARVEST

As stated before, Ishmael ministries seem to be more fruitful than Isaac ministries when both ministries are immature, just as Hagar seemed to be more fruitful than Sarah. Sarah was barren, and yet God used this barren woman as the mother of Isaac, the mother who brought forth the son of promise. Likewise, in the last days, Isaac will be much more fruitful than Ishmael. Ishmael's time of prominence is coming to an end while Isaac's is just beginning.

The complete fulfillment of the prophecy of Isaac will be fulfilled during the final harvest. As Paul writes about Ishmael and Isaac in Galatians 4, he quotes the following prophecy: It is written **"Rejoice, O barren, you who do not bear! break forth and shout, you who are not in labor! for the desolate has many more children than she who has a husband"** (4:27). In the same way, Isaac ministries, the offspring of barren Sarah, will have many more children than Ishmael ministries in the last days.

CASTING OUT ISHMAEL

Paul also reminds us of what must become of Ishmael as Isaac arises.

> **Now we, brethren, as Isaac was, are children of promise. But, as he who was born according to the flesh then persecuted him who was born according to the Spirit, even so it is now. Nevertheless what does the Scripture say? "CAST OUT THE BONDWOMAN AND HER SON, FOR THE SON OF THE BONDWOMAN SHALL NOT BE HEIR WITH THE SON OF THE FREEWOMAN." So then, brethren, we are not children of the bondwoman but of the free. (Galatians 4:28-31)**

There is a ministry taking shape in the earth that will fulfill the promises of God. This ministry is very different from the churches and ministries that we know today. It is not built by the mind of men, or the hands of men. It is not a ministry run according to administrative principles. It is the house of God. It is run by the sons of God, led by the Spirit of God.

This ministry is led by men who have passed through the fire, just like the early apostles. These leaders are men who no longer trust in their own wisdom and insight. They are men who have been broken, men who have learned to walk very closely with the lord. They no longer care about the expectations of religious men. They only care about the voice of their Father.

When this ministry arises, Ishmael will mock it. Ishmael believes that he is the one to fulfill the Lord's promise. Ishmael believes that if God would do something, it would surely be done through him.

And so there must come a separation between Ishmael and Isaac. If there is no separation, Ishmael will take on the heart of Cain, the heart of the cuckoo bird. He will become so jealous, so sure that he is the chosen son, the chosen ministry, that he will try to kill his brother.

This is the dividing line. When established ministries mock and despise the ministries that God himself is birthing, the line has been crossed.   Many established churches feel it is their God-given right to mock and despise new moves of God.   They automatically assume that they can judge, critique, and condemn a move of the Spirit that is still in its infancy, that is not yet established.   They do this because they feel so sure of their position.

They do not realize that they have taken on the heart of the cuckoo bird.   They believe that the thing God is bringing to life is illegitimate and that they themselves are legitimate.   They do not realize that they have become very religious and that they are judging according to the flesh and not by the spirit.   They do not realize that they are opposing the work of God.   They do not realize that they are being led by the spirit of Cain, the spirit of religion, and not by the Spirit of the Lord.

In the coming move of God, there is no room for established churches and movements to become the enemy of what God is doing.   That time is over.   He will not allow it.   For many years God has blessed and tolerated Ishmael.   Now, when Ishmael uses that very blessing as evidence that he is allowed to attack what is new, it will bring judgment upon him.

Those who hold on to their religious systems during the final harvest will be judged together with those systems, just as the Pharisees and their religion were swept away in the first century.   Those who set their hearts to truly know God and follow Him will discover that a great door is opened for them.

In this separation, many ministries that seemed impressive according to natural human standards are being displaced.   They are being removed from their place.   They are losing favor with God and man. They are being sent to the desert as God raises up Isaac.

The Lord is in the desert, waiting for Ishmael.   If Ishmael humbles himself, he will receive grace. He will receive the water of God's Word, which will restore his soul and give him new life.   If Ishmael humbles himself and seeks the Lord in the desert, God will raise him up again as a son of God. Some Ishmael ministries will be restored and used during the end time harvest.   Others will become so embittered, so filled with rejection, that they will die in the desert.

VAUGHN MARTIN

8 MOURNING FOR THE CHILDREN

TRUSTING THE CHURCH WITH YOUR CHILDREN

Eli Brubaker grew up in a staunch Mennonite family. He married a Mennonite wife, raised his family in the Mennonite Church, and sent his children to the local Mennonite school. He was a model citizen in the community. He worked hard, gave generously, and excelled in his business as a building contractor.

Eli and his wife Esther never gave much thought to the schools where they sent their children. Most people in his church sent their children to the local Mennonite schools, and he and his wife did likewise. They attended Lancaster Mennonite High School, where they were surrounded by Mennonites, protected by the cocoon of Mennonite culture and faith.

Naturally the next step was to the Mennonite colleges. Eli's daughter Sandy chose Goshen. Eli's firstborn son Robert chose Eastern Mennonite University. Only the youngest son, Doug, chose to attend a secular university, Penn State.

Eli's children were committed Christians. Sandy accepted the Lord during a summer camp at the Camp Hebron, a camp closely associated with the Mennonite faith. Robert and his brother also accepted the Lord as young men. They all became baptized members of the Mennonite Church.

When Robert told Eli that he had decided to attend Eastern Mennonite University instead of a secular university, Eli felt proud of his son's commitment to the Mennonite faith.

Eli testified later that he didn't really understand what was taking place. Nobody in his Mennonite circle of friends ever warned him that it might not be the best thing for his children to attend a Mennonite college. Nobody warned him what could happen. Everybody just sent their children to the Mennonite schools and colleges without much worry.

Robert seemed to do well at EMU, where he studied biology and chemistry. He continued dating his high school sweetheart. He kept a good relationship with his parents, sometimes sending them letters thanking them for being his parents. It was only later on that Eli realized that Robert was taught things at EMU that went against the belief system that he grew up with.

Sandy, Eli's second born, chose Goshen College because of its nursing program. Eli and Esther still remember the day that they took Sandy to Goshen, where they met with the college's representatives who gave them an introduction to the college. One of the professors who met with the parents that day told them plainly, "Your child better know what she believes when she comes here because we are going to challenge those beliefs." Eli was troubled by these words. He was sending his daughter to a Mennonite school because he hoped that a Mennonite school would reinforce the values and training that he had been giving his children. Now here was a college representative telling him point blank on their first day of meeting that the school would do its best to tear down the foundations that were laid.

When Eli spoke out his concerns to the college representative, the representative replied with condescension: "Oh, you come from

Lancaster County, Pennsylvania. You Lancaster County Mennonites have your heads in the sand." He told them that the things they were concerned about really weren't important. What was important was the social gospel, helping the oppressed.

At that moment, Eli and Esther wanted to put Sandy back in their van and return her to Pennsylvania. They had a sense that her time at Goshen would go horribly wrong. And yet their daughter was so excited about her college. Taking her home would have set off a family crisis. Her parents gave in to her wishes, a decision they later regretted.

Sandy lost something at Goshen. She entered the school a committed Christian. A few years later, she received her nursing degree. Today, Sandy's parents aren't sure exactly what she believes, but they fear that she has turned away from biblical Christianity. They fear that she was deeply influenced by the open-minded, left-wing campus Christianity that she experienced at Goshen. She got married and then divorced and doesn't presently attend any church.

Robert seemed to be holding on to his faith, but there were indications that all was not well. When it came time for Eli's youngest son Doug to choose a college, Doug was concerned that he wouldn't find committed Christians at his chosen college, Penn State University.

Robert reassured his brother Doug. "I am sure you will find much better Bible study groups at Penn State than you would find at Eastern Mennonite University," he told him. In fact, Robert was right. Doug did find a group of committed Christians at Penn State, and he was the only one of the Brubaker children to graduate from college with his faith intact.

Robert, meanwhile, began walking a darker path. He left college, his Mennonite girlfriend, and eventually the Christian faith entirely. He started studying other religions as he began a relationship with a woman from a Hindu background. He began struggling with alcohol addiction.

Eli and Esther watched with deep grief what was happening to their children. Eli realized that the faith of his children was destroyed in the

Mennonite schools. He felt foolish and naïve and betrayed. He had been so trusting of his church and its institutions, and in return they destroyed his family. He wishes that he had sent his children to public schools and colleges, instead of Mennonite ones. He thinks he could have helped them to hold on to their faith and stand for their faith more easily in a public institution than in a Mennonite one.

Eli went through a personal spiritual renewal as he sought the Lord for his children. He had a powerful encounter with God one day as he was reading and praying over the Scripture. As he read the Scripture about loving the Lord your God with all your might, it was like the Lord was speaking to him. Eli lifted weights, and a weight lifter pushes his strength to the absolute limit as he strives with all his might to complete his final rep. Eli felt the Lord telling him that he needs to love the Lord with that same intensity. Eli began to spend three hours a night in prayer and Bible study. The Lord met with Eli and spoke to him. It became a precious time for him.

Eli's children continued to walk away from the Lord, and Eli and Esther continued praying for them. In 2017 Robert called Eli in tears. He had had an experience that shook him to his core. He had seen hell. In tears and terror he said to Eli, "Dad, I saw hell. It was so terrible. I can't even begin to describe how terrible hell is. I never want to go there!"

Robert began to confess the wrongs he had committed against his parents. He begged his father's forgiveness for things he had done and said. He stopped drinking.

Eli and Esther believe that God is sovereignly reaching out to their son and pulling him off of the road that leads to destruction. They believe that God will answer their prayer for Sandy also.

Some people have heard so much about God's love that they no longer take the message seriously. Such people need to understand that both heaven and hell are very, very real, and that there is only one way to escape the coming judgment.

MOURN FOR THE CHILDREN, NOT THE INSTITUTIONS

It is time for judgment to begin in the house of the Lord. Ishmael and Cain are being removed from their place of influence and prestige. They are losing their position as first-born sons. They are being driven into the desert. God will not allow them to murder His children.

The American religious institutions that dominate American Christianity are in a process of crumbling. They will crumble because of external pressures such as lawsuits and unfriendly governmental regulations. They will crumble because they are rotten on the inside. They will crumble because God is releasing judgment upon them.

Most of all, they will crumble because the sons of God are beginning to rise. God is doing something awesome in our day. A complete transformation of the church is taking place. Everything that was built for the glory of man, by the religious mind of man, is crumbling. Everything that pretends to be of God but is just the imitation is being exposed. At the same time, the sons of God are coming forth.

The Lord spoke to me and told me that He is bringing an end to the religious systems of men. He told me that when these systems are destroyed, I should not mourn for the system. Instead, he told me to mourn for the children who were destroyed in that system.

In the Mennonite church, generations of parents have sent their children to the Mennonite colleges just as Eli Brubaker did. They sent their children to these schools because it was the thing to do in the churches that they attended. Everything seemed so familiar and safe.

Unfortunately, the schools were controlled by the hijackers, the cuckoo birds of religion. Thousands of young Christians who attended these educational institutions had their faith destroyed. The story of Eli Brubaker is extremely common. Every Mennonite who reads this book is likely to know several similar stories just among his own set of friends and acquaintances. Even Mennonite readers who are not happy with my sweeping denunciations of the Mennonite colleges are likely to know at least several friends who lost their faith in the Mennonite educational institutions. I am not exaggerating the problem. The reality is far worse than this book is able to express.

Jesus said that if anyone causes one of the little ones who believe in Him to stumble, it would be better for him if a millstone were hung around his neck, and he were thrown into the depths of the sea (Matthew 18:6). The great sin of the Mennonite educational institutions is that they cause the little ones to stumble. They cause young Christians to lose their faith in Christ. They try to convert these young Christians to the religion of the campuses, the left-wing campus Christianity that replaces the knowledge of the living Christ with a lot of politically correct drivel.

For some, this time of separation is a time of suffering. It was not easy for Abraham to separate from Ishmael and send him into the desert. It was not easy for Adam to see his son Cain sent into the desert. But Adam had a son Seth and Abraham had Isaac. If these fathers had not rid their nests of the cuckoo birds, the cuckoo birds would surely have murdered their other children.

We are in a time where Ishmael and Cain are being judged. Therefore, every person and every ministry must separate himself from these things if he hopes to be part of what God is doing. This means different things for different people. For some, it means they must pull out of denominations and religious institutions that are dominated by the spirit of religion. These can be very liberal, left wing institutions or very conservative, traditional institutions. It doesn't matter if religion is left wing or very conservative. Religion kills. Religion is the cuckoo bird.

If Mennonites do not leave these institutions, they will lose their children. Children who are raised in these institutions are destroyed by the cuckoo birds of religion. They are destroyed by the college professors who think it is their God-given duty to undermine and attack the simple biblical faith of their students. The children's lives are destroyed by the spiritual culture of these institutions, where anything that is holy is mocked and where sexual perversion is celebrated. If you want your children to live, get them out before it is too late.

Meanwhile, there are many churches that are part of denominational structures that are completely controlled by the spirits of religion, especially the religion of political correctness and left-wing campus Christianity. Many of these congregations want to obey the Lord. They want to be led by the Holy Spirit. They don't want to waste their time arguing about such things as gay marriage. They know that sin is sin. These churches must leave these structures if they desire to remain spiritually alive. If they stay connected to these larger organizations, perhaps hoping that they will influence them in a positive direction, it is they who will be influenced. Instead of spending their time seeking the Lord and reaching their community with the gospel of Jesus Christ, they will waste their time arguing about whether or not the foundational doctrines of Christianity are actually true. They will waste their time arguing about whether or not clearly sinful activity is actually sinful.

Time is short. Now is not the time to be arguing about foolishness with religious people who will never change. Now is the time to preach the gospel to a lost and hurting world. Now is the time to demonstrate the power of God on the streets. If you spend all your time arguing with the religious, you will waste your life and your energy.

Finally, it is necessary to look inwards to see if Ishmael is in you. Are you being led by the Holy Spirit or by religion? How do you make your decisions? So much of what people think is God is just the voice of their own minds or the voice of religion.

I lead a missionary training school in East Africa. At that school, we seek the Lord for hour after hour, until He speaks. We try to do this for every major decision. Before we send a team into an unreached Muslim community, we might spend days or even weeks praying and worshiping with that team. In fact, there is no timeline. We simply will not send them unless we are sure that the Lord Himself is the one sending them. And when the Lord speaks, whether it is after one day of prayer or after three months of prayer, we take action. The team goes in faith, believing that the Lord will open doors for them in that community.

These teams do not try to open doors in that community using natural human methods, the ways of Ishmael. They don't dig wells or give gifts in hopes that the community will open its doors to them. They go with nothing except the Gospel of Jesus Christ and the power of God. They look for the man of peace that God has prepared for them. They pray for the sick and preach the good news of the kingdom.

The doors always open. When someone is sent by the Lord Himself and he goes in faith and boldness, God always makes a way. Miracles happen frequently. Sometimes the Muslims are ready to receive the messengers of the kingdom because they have been receiving dreams and visions of Jesus.

It has been a wonderful time of working to train and send African missionaries. And yet, in spite of all the testimonies and miracles, I know that our ministry is still a mixture of Ishmael and Isaac. I know that we too, need to separate ourselves from Ishmael. There is a level of the supernatural power and a level of supernatural love that we have not yet attained. I know that God will raise up teams that are much more wholehearted, much more focused on the prize. I know that these teams will cut through the Islamic strongholds like a hot knife through butter. I know that as they demonstrate the kingdom of heaven, the kingdom of Islam will be exposed for the demonic religion that it is. I know that as the servants of God move in fearlessness and supernatural boldness, the intimidation of Islam will be broken off communities, and entire communities will begin to turn to Christ.

This is the beginning of the final harvest. Islam is falling, and with it every religious system of man is being judged. This is true in the "Christian" religion, the world religions and in the realm of the cults and pagan religions that turn up here and there.

It shall come to pass in the last days that **"the mountain of the LORD's house shall be established on the top of the mountains, And shall be exalted above the hills; And all nations shall flow to it. Many people shall come and say, "Come, and let us go up to the mountain of the LORD, To the house of the God of Jacob;**

**He will teach us His ways, And we shall walk in His paths."
(Isaiah 2:2-3)**

The "mountain of the LORD's house" is his kingdom. The mountains represent the world's religions, and the hills the cults and smaller religious systems. The Lord's kingdom will be established above the mountains and hills, above the cults. Every religion will be exposed. Every nation will receive a powerful testimony that Jesus is alive.

At this moment, many Christians feel overwhelmed by the spread of the religion of political correctness in America. They see the vast majority of Christian schools being hijacked by the cuckoo birds of religion. They see the educated elite of their denominations graduating from those schools with unbiblical and unchristian views on many subjects. They see the millennial generation abandoning their Christian faith.

They feel the overwhelming hostility of the secular media, who seem to think that evangelical Christians are a half- step away from being neo-Nazis. They turn on their televisions and see the stream of ungodly filth broadcast on hundreds of channels, 24 hours a day. They feel the legal pressure from those who want to push biblical Christianity and Bible-believing Christians out of nearly every part of society.

Christians view this hatred, this hostility against Christ in our culture, and they decide that the war is lost. Some are deciding that it is no longer possible to see America change in a positive direction. They believe that the fight for American culture is over and that it is better to retreat into closed religious communities.

THE BENEDICT OPTION
Rod Dreher recently published a bestseller titled *The Benedict Option*. In this book Dreher encourages Christians to follow the example of the Roman Catholic monk Benedict, who left the ruins of Rome to create a religious community that would keep the faith alive until the day that civilization could be rebuilt. Dreher believes that Christians need to fight using a "strategic retreat," forming communities that can hold their ground against the onslaught of an aggressively secular society,

holding on to the positive parts of our Christian heritage as we wait for a better day. Dreher advocates homeschooling, turning off the television, and other ways of cutting off the influence of mainstream cultural influence so as to rebuild Christian communities.

Dreher undoubtedly gives some good advice. Nevertheless, it is probably doomed to failure. Withdrawing from society seems like a good solution when society is trying to crush everything a person holds dear. But forming communities that are set apart and separate from the world doesn't always work out very well. Rebecca Weiss writes about the attempt of her father to form such a community:

> ....Because, you see, the Benedict Option – though not by that name – was around for a good forty years before Dreher sat down to write. My father was one of several who came up with the idea. While running a raucous bar in Chapel Hill, NC, he was also reading Thomas Merton and Louis Bromfield and Ralph Waldo Emerson, and eventually came to the conclusion that the best bet for Christians in the modern world was to come out and "be set apart." He even drew on his understanding of St. Benedict's communities, with a special stress on the notion of "ora et labora." Because my father opted actually to do the thing, instead of sitting in an office writing a book about it, you have never heard of him. Which means, I suppose, that his attempt was fairly successful. But these attempts are never all that successful.
>
> And there are other problems: when you try to come Out (or In?), whatever you feared in the World comes in with you, into your microcosm. It's ironic that my father's first community was called "New Eden." Into every Eden, a serpent will come. We tend to bring it in with us. Want to escape from overweening tyrannical power? Too bad, you probably brought it with you, and you will find the community dominated by whichever leader (usually male) has the loudest voice and the least empathy. Want to escape from sexual perversion? Ha. Have I got some stories! It's amazing just how perverse people can be, on the land, when no one is looking. Want to escape from a welfare system in which those who don't work won't eat? I can assure you, you will be shelling beans or building a cabin while nearby some hanger-on rambles on forever

about how misunderstood he is. Tired of nitpicking bureaucracy? Your community will be filled with nitpickers, happy to call you out if your daughters' skirts are too short, or if your sons have been listening to evil music like (gasp) Simon and Garfunkel. [15]

Of course, nobody knows more about forming communities that are separate from the world than the Mennonites and Amish. And nobody knows better than Mennonites and Amish just how toxic closed communities can become. As Rebecca writes, "When you try to come Out (or In?), whatever you feared in the World comes in with you, into your microcosm. It's ironic that my father's first community was called "New Eden." Into every Eden, a serpent will come. We tend to bring it in with us…"

In other words, what takes place in closed religious communities can be just as bad, or even worse, as what takes place in the world. People who leave these communities often give the same testimony: that what the world sees on the outside of these communities is not what is taking place on the inside. The amount of hidden sin that takes place in these communities is shocking. There are many reports of child abuse and sexual molestation taking place in Old Order Amish communities.

And of course, there is the religion. Many of these communities seemed to be ruled by the letter of the law instead of by the Holy Spirit. The most controlling, religious men often gain dominant positions in these communities, and they use their power to control the lives of everyone.

Many who are extremely hostile to religion today had very negative experiences in closed religious communities. Some found no life in those communities but just a joyless, rigid, judgmental form of religion. Some witnessed sexual abuse taking place that was covered up by religious leaders. Some experienced heavy-handed control, manipulation, and hypocrisy that embittered them against every expression of religious faith.

---

[15] http://www.patheos.com/blogs/suspendedinherjar/2017/04/family-benedict-option-cool-heres-doesnt-work/

FAITH MENNONITE HIGH SCHOOL

I grew up in a conservative Mennonite family. Our family was somewhat unique, because my father, although a conservative Mennonite, was also a psychiatrist. It is difficult to imagine a more secular, humanistic world than the world of 1970s psychiatry. Yet even as his career advanced in psychiatry, my father remained a conservative Mennonite. He became a pastor and later a Mennonite bishop.

As we grew up, my father was worried that we would lose our faith. We attended public schools, but my parents imposed a certain kind of dress code upon us. It was a big step when they allowed me to wear shorts for gym class. My sisters all wore the Mennonite head covering as their mother did.

At one moment, my parents decided that we should attend a very conservative Mennonite school known as Faith Mennonite High School. Faith Mennonite was attended by conservative Mennonites and Beachy Amish. It was required for the girls to wear the head covering. Many wore the traditional Mennonite cape dresses that were designed to hide the female figure.

Faith Mennonite was designed to be a safe place, a place where the moral influences of the surrounding world would not enter. It took quite a sacrifice to attend Faith. We needed to drive nearly an hour every morning and evening to arrive there. We went in a vanload filled with the children of Mennonite families who had similar concerns to our parents.

At Faith Mennonite, there was chapel every morning. The boys took practical classes in subjects such as welding, woodworking and electrical installation in addition to their regular classes. The girls took classes in baking and homemaking.

Everyone at the school was some flavor of Mennonite or Amish. Everything was focused on creating a religious community that would be faithful to the Lord and the Scriptures. In some ways Faith Mennonite seemed like a successful attempt to escape the influence of the world.

Nevertheless, the world entered. I remember the morning chapel service in which the secretary got up and confessed in floods of tears that she was involved in an inappropriate relationship with the principal. At first the secretary and principal maintained that they had simply been inappropriate with one another. Soon the full story came out, and their affair was exposed.

The attitude of the students went from bad to worse. The young men became openly rebellious against the school administration. They talked of secret parties and alcohol and other vices. One friend of mine visited the school after hours one day. He managed to get the double doors opened. He backed his pickup truck into the hallways and burned rubber up and down the halls.

My parents recognized that the atmosphere at Faith Mennonite High school was becoming worse. They began to fear that I would rebel against the school and against Christianity. They decided that it was better for me to attend the local public school. None of us ever regretted that decision. Faith Mennonite eventually recovered from the events of that year. Today it continues its educational mission of teaching necessary academic courses and the Word of God to conservative Mennonite high school students.

One of my classmates at Faith Mennonite was Theda Good. When I knew her, Theda was a friendly, outgoing girl. Quite simply, she seemed like one of the nicest people in the school. Briefly she dated a friend of mine. She seemed to be a very committed Christian. In 2014 Theda became the first person to receive her ministry license in a Mennonite church while involved in a lesbian relationship.

RETREAT IS NO OPTION
The point is this: retreating into a closed religious community is not the answer. Many Mennonites moved from a conservative form of religion to a liberal form of religion during the past four decades. Now, as liberal Mennonite churches are moving away from biblical Christianity, some think that we need to move towards a more conservative form of religion, back into closed religious communities.

Moving from one religion to another is not the answer. The judgment that is coming upon the religious systems is being released against both conservative and liberal forms of religion. Left wing campus Christianity is being judged by God. The conservative Mennonite religion is also being judged.

The truth is that often the conservative Mennonite religion is not led by the Spirit of God any more than the liberal Mennonite religion is. The conservatives are led by the laws and rules created by religious men. The systems of religion lack resurrection life and power.

There is only one solution. There is a battle taking place between the sons of God and the sons of religion. As many as are led by the Spirit of God, these are the sons of God (Romans 8:14). God is raising up a people who are not religious. He is raising up a people who actually know Him. They know His voice and His power. They know the difference between the laws created by religious men and the holiness of the living God.

In fact, the church is going through something that is like a death and a resurrection. The religious systems are being judged. Many things are coming to an end. Many things that seemed stable and secure are shaking and will soon crumble. At the same time, God is raising up something beautiful out of the ashes. May His kingdom come, and His will be done, on earth, even in America, just as it is in heaven.

9 ESCAPING RELIGION

THE WAR IN HEAVEN

There is a war taking place between the sons of God, and the sons of religion. This war will determine the fate of this planet. As long as the devil is able to keep the sons of religion in their position, this planet remains under his control.

God created man to rule and reign with Him over this planet. The Bible says that God created thrones, dominions, principalities, and powers (Colossians 1:16). They were created through Him and for Him. In other words, just as our nation has different divisions of political authority, such as townships, counties, and states, each with their own government, something similar exists in the spiritual realm. In the spiritual realm, there are thrones, dominions, principalities, and powers.

If God created spiritual thrones over the earth, whom did he intend to sit on these thrones? The teachings of Paul and Jesus himself make it clear that at the present time, the evil one rules over the earth. Paul writes in Ephesians 6:12: **"We wrestle not against flesh and blood but against principalities and powers against the rulers of the darkness of this age, against spiritual hosts of wickedness in the heavenly places."** **Jesus called the devil the ruler of this world** (John 12:31).

The devil's agents sit on their spiritual thrones ruling the earth. Is this what God intended? Of course not. God did not create the devil and his angels to rule over the earth in rebellion against Him. God created man to rule and reign with Him. He created man, in His image, in His likeness, and said "let them have dominion..." God is Spirit, and we are created in His likeness. God intended man to have a spiritual dominion over the earth. He created man to rule and reign with Him.

The devil's legal right to rule this earth is found in one way only – he has convinced men to turn over their authority to him. He has convinced men to form blood covenants with him, in which everything that they have is given to him. This is why the devil could say to Jesus, "These kingdoms have been given to me..." (Luke 4:6). When he said this to Jesus, he had the evidence to back up what he was saying; he had the title deeds to the kingdoms of the earth.

These title deeds consisted of all the covenants that men have made with him. Many religious rituals involve covenant with the devil. Every ritual of the secret societies involve covenant. These covenants turn over man's legal rights to the Evil One.

And so, in the spiritual realm that is connected to this fallen earth, there are an abundance of evil rulers. These rulers are connected by covenant to fallen mankind. These rulers sit on the spiritual thrones that were intended for mankind.

When Jesus rose from the dead, he defeated every evil force, every fallen angel, every principality and power, and the devil himself. He rose up through the heavens and is seated at the right hand of the Father. Nevertheless, although he defeated these evil forces, he allowed them to continue their rule over the earth for a time. He allowed them to remain until the saints overcome.

In Revelation 12 we read about war taking place in the heavenly realms. We read about Michael and his angels fighting against the devil and his angels. The Bible tells us that there was no longer room found in heaven for the devil and his angels. God orders Michael and his angels to cast the devil and his angels out of their seats of authority, down to the earth.

This great victory is not the victory of Jesus. When the Bible speaks of this victory, it doesn't say, "Jesus overcame." It says, "They overcame by the blood of the Lamb, by the word of their testimony, and they didn't love their lives unto death" (Revelation 12:11).

Why doesn't this verse say, "Jesus overcame..."? Jesus has already overcome. He has already defeated every evil spiritual being. He is seated at the right hand of the father. But he has allowed these evil spirits to remain ruling over the earth until the saints overcome. When the saints overcome, there will no longer be room in the heavenly realms for the devil and his angels. These devils are seated on the thrones intended for the saints. When the saints overcome "by the blood of the Lamb by the word of their testimony, and by not loving their lives to the death", they are proving that they belong completely to the Lord. They are proving that they have no covenant with the Evil One. They are proving that they love God more than their own life. They are proving that they are ready to sit on the thrones in the heavenly realms, ruling with Christ. When God sees these saints, these overcomers, these sons of God, he gives the instruction to Michael, "Michael, get rid of these devils who are ruling over the earth. My sons are arising to rule and reign with me. These devils are sitting on their thrones. There is no longer room for these devils in the heavenly places, because my sons are arising."

Can you understand why the devil is trying to stop the rise of these sons? Can you understand why he does everything in his power to keep the sons of man from seeing God and obeying God? Can you understand why the title of the devil in this passage is "the accuser of the brethren"? He accuses the saints of God day and night before the throne. He tells God, "These Christians, who pretend to follow you…they are hypocrites. They are committing sexual immorality. They are following me and not you. They are forming blood covenants in their religious rituals that prove that they belong to me. They are forming blood covenants as they commit sexual immorality, acts which prove that they belong to me. They are connected to me. They are mine. If you kick me out and cast me into hell, you have to cast them out with me."

This is why God allows the devil to remain in authority. Because he has formed covenants with mankind; he is connected to mankind. If God casts the devil out of this earth into the pit today, he would have to cast out his covenant partners with him. He would have to condemn mankind together with the devil.

This is why God did not immediately cast the devil into the pit when Jesus rose from the dead. He allowed him to remain until the saints are ready to replace him. He has allowed the devil to remain until the overcomers rise up.

The overcomers overcome by proving that they love God more than their life. They overcome by the blood of the lamb, which represents the covenant that believers have with the living God. This covenant is not one-sided. Not only did Jesus give his life for us, He tells us that if we follow Him, we must deny ourselves and take up our cross and follow after Him. This is why the overcomers overcome by the blood, by their testimony, and by not loving their lives to the death. They overcome by obeying God even when it might cost them their lives.

When overcomers arise, they displace every evil spiritual authority. When overcomers arise, they are not walking in any sort of false covenant with the evil one. They have one covenant, the covenant with the living God. They give their lives to that covenant. The devil has no hold on them, no connection to them. They become unstoppable.

When the overcomers arise, completely obeying the Lord, the devil will be cast down. He will completely lose his authority. He will rage upon the earth for a short time and then be cast into the pit.

THE GLORIOUS LIBERTY OF THE SONS OF GOD

These overcomers are the sons of God. The Bible teaches us that all creation is waiting with earnest expectation for the sons of God to be revealed. These sons will deliver creation from its bondage to the evil one. These sons will lead all creation into the glorious liberty of the sons of God.

For if you live according to the flesh you will die; but if by the Spirit you put to death the deeds of the body, you will live. For as many as are led by the Spirit of God, these are sons of God. For you did not receive the spirit of bondage again to fear, but you received the Spirit of adoption by whom we cry out, "Abba, Father." The Spirit Himself bears witness with our spirit that we are children of God, and if children, then heirs—heirs of God and joint heirs with Christ, if indeed we suffer with *Him,* that we may also be glorified together.

For I consider that the sufferings of this present time are not worthy *to be compared* with the glory which shall be revealed in us. For the earnest expectation of the creation eagerly waits for the revealing of the sons of God. For the creation was subjected to futility, not willingly, but because of Him who subjected *it* in hope; because the creation itself also will be delivered from the bondage of corruption into the glorious liberty of the children of God. For we know that the whole creation groans and labors with birth pangs together until now (Romans 8:13-22).

The sons of God are free. They are completely free. There is no demonic bondage associated with them in any way. They are free of fear. They are free of greed. The sins of the flesh have no hold on them at all. They are free to live their lives the way God intended for them to live.

It might seem strange that the ones who are obedient unto death are the most free beings on this planet, but it is true. In their deception, men think that freedom is about obeying the lusts of their flesh. A "free" man lusts after a woman, so he breaks his covenant with his wife and commits sexual immorality. A "free" man lusts after the high that drugs give him, so he puts everything in his life at risk just to get that high.

In reality, the one who obeys the lusts of the flesh ends up in slavery, not freedom. These lusts never lead people to freedom. Just as the man who craves ice cream will begin to carry extra weight around if he submits to that craving, the man who obeys the lust of the flesh will come under the burden and bondage of sin.

In contrast, there are deeper desires hidden in the heart than the lusts of the flesh. God has created mankind to know Him and worship Him, to walk with Him and rule with Him over creation. This desire to truly have relationship with God, to truly love God, is hidden in every human heart.

Unfortunately, it is not easy to reach the depths of a man's heart. My African friend Katana compares the human heart to a coconut. He says that the inside of the coconut is sweet and good to eat, but it is covered by a hard shell. In the same way, deep within every heart of man there is something that was created to know God and love God. This deep inner desire is closed off by a hard shell. The shell of the coconut represents all the hurts and wounds that men receive. It represents the bondages of the heart, the bondages to the sins of the flesh.

This shell of the coconut can also be compared to religion. In religion, men think they are serving God. In fact, when a man obeys religious spirits, his heart never connects to God. He goes through the motions of his religion, but it impossible for his heart to truly connect to God through religion.

RELIGIOUS RITUALS

There is a calling so high and so awesome that the flesh of man recoils from it. When Scripture says, "Be ye therefore holy as God is holy" (I Peter 1:16), it is calling people to an inner transformation so complete that they become unrecognizable. The flesh of man recoils from this calling, even as the deepest part of a man's spirit yearns to be one with the living God.

God's holiness is beyond our comprehension. The seraphim see this holiness and cover their faces and feet as they cry out continually, "Holy, Holy, Holy is the Lord God almighty, who was, and is, and is to come " (Isaiah 6:2).

This holiness of God is so complete and so pure that it is frightening to men. Therefore men try to create their own form of holiness. They create a holiness that they can control, a holiness that is not so intimidating. Men form dress codes and rules for living. They forbid many things. They think their codes of behavior are holy.

These codes of behavior are found in many religions. They restrict the lawlessness of people to some degree, but they cannot change a person's heart. Only the supernatural power of God can change the heart.

In the end, these codes of behavior lead people in circles. They do not lead people to the living God. All the laws and rules of the Pharisees did not lead them closer to God. Religion feeds the flesh of a person and satisfies that flesh with rituals that seem to be good but lead nowhere.

WHAT IS A SON OF GOD?

The key to being an overcomer is to walk with the Lord in covenant, speaking His Word even if it costs your life. The key to being a son of God is essentially the same. "As many as are led by the Spirit of God, these are the sons of God" (Romans 8:14). The sons of God led by the Spirit of God take action, not according to the voices of men or the voices of religion, but according to the Spirit of God. They are led by the Spirit of God.

THE VOICES OF RELIGION, MONEY, AND FAMILY

If you want to obey the voice of the Holy Spirit and walk in unity with a holy God, you must learn to recognize that voice, and you must reject all the other voices that will try to direct your life. Religion has a voice. If you obey the voice of religion, it will be impossible for you to obey the Lord. Money has a voice. If you obey the voice of money, it will be impossible for you to obey the Spirit of God. Your family has a voice. If you completely obey the voice of your family, it will not be possible for you to completely obey the Lord. Your friends and associates have a voice. If you completely obey them, you will not completely obey the Lord.

Perhaps the most difficult voice to disobey on this list is the voice of family. Every person has family obligations. Children are instructed to obey their parents. They are not supposed to ignore the voice of their parents. Paul says that a man who does not care for his family is worse than an unbeliever (I Timothy 5:8). It is wrong for a man to ignore the needs of his family. Wives are called to submit to their husbands. It would be wrong for a wife to ignore her husband's wishes.

At the same time, if a man allows his life to be completely directed by the voice of his family, it will be impossible for him to completely obey God. A wife respects and honors her husband and even obeys him in many things. A child obeys his parents. And yet, there are certain moments in life in which one must disobey his family if he desires to obey God. If you always obey your parents, what will happen when your parents have a different plan for your life than the plan that God has? Which plan will you follow? Is the plan that your parents have for you the same as the plan that God has for you?

CHILDREN OBEY YOUR PARENTS
When I got married, my father spoke some very wise words to me. He said to me, "Son, when you were a child, you were required to obey me. The Bible says, 'Children, obey your parents.' Today you are no longer a child. You are a man, and you need to make decisions for yourself and your family. The Bible says, 'Honor your father and mother, that your days might be long.' You always need to honor me, but from this day forward you no longer need to obey me, because you are no longer a child."

How can you as a grown adult honor your parents? You can honor them by focusing on what is honorable about them. When you speak about your parents, you speak about their good qualities and not their bad ones. You honor the good example that they have set. You never despise them or speak badly about them.

At the same time, as an adult, understand that one day you will give an account before God for your life. It will not be good enough for you to say on that day, "I lived my life the way my parents wanted me to." On that day you will stand before God, and you will give an account for your decisions in life. Did you obey the voice of God or disobey Him? Did you follow the voice of the Holy Spirit or the voice of your family?

Is it possible to honor your father and mother without obeying them? I believe it is. There came a time in Jesus' life where he disobeyed the wishes of his parents. He remained in Jerusalem, discussing the law with the religious leaders there, while his parents assumed that he should come home with them. They expressed their displeasure to Jesus, who replied to them, "Didn't you know I needed to be about my Father's business?" (Luke 2:49)

There was a time when the mother and brothers of Jesus came to him insisting that he leave what he was doing and return home with them. Jesus was doing the work of His Father in heaven, and yet his earthly mother thought that she could control his life. Jesus did not accept Mary's attempt to control him. He said "Who are my mother and brothers? They are the ones who do the will of my Father who is in heaven" (Mark 3:33-34).

One of the disciples of Jesus said to him, "Lord I will follow you, but first let me go and bury my father...." Attending your father's funeral seems like a very legitimate responsibility for a son. What kind of son would refuse to attend his father's own funeral? What could be more important in life than the funeral of one's own father? Jesus answered, "Follow me and let the dead bury their own dead."

A funeral is not just a normal meeting. The days that surround a funeral are also the days in which family business is settled. Who will take care of relatives left behind when the father has died? Who will take care of Mother? How will the inheritance be divided? Who will take ownership of the family business? The voice of family responsibility is very strong in such a setting.

Jesus knew just how powerful the voice of one's family is. He knew that if his disciple attended the funeral, the voice of family would be too strong for him. If his disciple attended the funeral of his father, the voice of family would take control of his life, and he would be unable to leave everything and follow Jesus. A burden of family responsibilities and expectations would be placed upon the man's shoulders, and he would be unable to follow Jesus while he carried that burden.

The sons of God must know the difference between the voice of family and the voice of the Lord. It is impossible to completely obey the voice of family and also to obey the Lord. There will be times in life that the voice of family must be disobeyed if one hopes to be led by the Spirit of the Lord.

Obviously, this statement can be misused. There are responsibilities of family that one must carry in order to be faithful to the Lord. Parents must take care of their children, and husbands and wives must be faithful to one another. Nevertheless, there are times when the voices of family give orders that one should not obey.

THE VOICE OF MONEY

Likewise, the sons of God must know the difference between the voice of money and the voice of the Lord. It is impossible to obey God and money.

Many, many lives are directed by money. Men listen to the voice of money, and they make their decisions in life. Money tells them where they should live and what career they should follow. Money tells them how far they should go in following Christ.

Money is a master. Money rules over the hearts and minds of men. Money rules with fear. Men fear what will happen if they do not obey money. Men fear that they won't have enough food to eat. They fear that they won't be able to live a good life. Jesus said, "No one can serve two masters. Either you will hate the one and love the other, or you will be devoted to the one and despise the other. You cannot serve both God and money." (Matthew 6:24)

Therefore, do not worry about anything! (Matthew 6:25-34) If money is not your God, then you will not worry about money! If money is not your master, then money will have no authority over you. You will not worry about what your master will do to you if you do not obey.

The man who is led by the Spirit of God cannot be led by money. Neither will he worry about money. He will make his decisions based upon the leading of the Holy Spirit. He will not make major decisions in life based upon the financial consequences of those decisions.

The man who is led by the Spirit of God will not worry about money or serve money. The man who is led by the Spirit of God uses money to serve the purposes of God and His kingdom. When this man enters into a business, he does so under the leading of the Holy Spirit. When he changes jobs, he doesn't do so because the new job makes more money than the old job. He changes his job because the Holy Spirit leads him to do so.

The Holy Spirit will not lead you to become lazy. The Holy Spirit will not cause you to stop providing for your family. The Holy Spirit will lead you on a good path, a path in which you become effective for the purposes of God, a path that is better than the path that you would have chosen for yourself.

The Holy Spirit will lead you on a path that doesn't always make sense according to human reasoning. Perhaps the Holy Spirit will lead you to take a job that seems to be a much less impressive opportunity than other job offers that you have received. And yet when you pray about the decision and lay it before the Lord, you receive the clear confirmation that He wants you to take the job that seems to be less impressive.

Perhaps there are people He wants you to minister to at your new job. Perhaps He will open up doors for your company so that it becomes far more influential than you expect. Perhaps He tells you the reasons for taking this job, perhaps He doesn't. Every act of obedience becomes an opportunity in life when you are actually obeying the voice of the Holy Spirit.

The key question is, who is leading you? What voice are you listening to? Do you simply take the job that offers the most money, or do you actually listen to what the Holy Spirit is saying?

THE VOICE OF FEAR

Another voice that directs the lives of men is the voice of fear. If you obey the voice of fear, it is impossible for you to obey the voice of the Lord. If you obey the voice of fear, you will become the slave of fear. You will live your life inside the box that fear sets for you.

The slaves of fear are not the sons of God. Those who obey the voice of the Lord must overcome their fear!

> **But the cowardly, unbelieving, abominable, murderers, sexually immoral, sorcerers, idolaters, and all liars shall have their part in the lake which burns with fire and brimstone, which is the second death. (Revelation 21:8)**

THE VOICE OF RELIGION

The most deceptive voice that people follow in the place of God is the voice of religion. Religion is the primary means that the devil uses to block people from the true presence and power of God. Religion deceives people into thinking that they are obeying the Spirit of God when actually they are just obeying religion. The Islamic terrorist believes he is obeying the Spirit of God, when in fact he is just obeying the spirit of the Islamic religion. The liberal Mennonite believes he is obeying the Spirit of God as he celebrates gay marriage. In fact, he is just obeying the spirit that inspires his religion, the spirit of the age. Likewise, a Pharisee believes that he is obeying God, as he follows the rules and regulations that come from the religious minds of people.

This is the evil of religion. Religion is the great imposter, the great deceiver, the one that takes the place of God and pretends to be God. As long as a man is obeying religion, he cannot obey God.

ACCEPT NO SUBSTITUTE

The voices of religion, family, money and fear order and direct the course of people's lives. Some men base every major decision on financial issues. They look at the costs and rewards of each path that they might take in life, and they make their decisions accordingly. These are the servants of money. Some men always obey the voice of family. They are sensitive to what their parents want them to do, to what their spouses want them to do, and to what their children want them to do. They are not sensitive to what the Holy Spirit is asking them to do. And some men do what they think God is asking them to do, but, in fact, it is not God who is speaking to them. These are the slaves of religion.

If you obey religion, you will enter increasing levels of bondage. In the final chapter of this book we will tell the sad story of a woman who wrapped herself in religion and entered into deep spiritual darkness. This is the blackness of religion, the realm of the Pharisees, the place where the blind lead the blind in futile circles. It is the domain of endless rules and laws that never lead men to God. It is a domain of jealousy and hatred towards the sons of God.

The sons of God are led by the Spirit of God. If this book puts anything in you, I pray that it puts in you a deep desire to actually know the voice of God and to follow that voice. Before you can follow that voice or hear that voice, it is necessary to silence the other voices. This is why when Jesus called his disciples, they left everything and followed him. They started life over, from the beginning. The voice of money was silenced as they left their possessions and businesses. The voice of family also lost its influence. And Jesus himself constantly confronted the Pharisees to keep the voice of religion from harming his flock.

THE OPINIONS OF MAN

One of the major obstacles to hearing the voice of the Lord is that people are so opinionated, so sure that they know what the Lord will say before He speaks. A religious man rarely has the patience to seek the Lord and wait upon His answer. He thinks he already knows the answer.

For example, consider two men who each want to buy a new car. One comes from a church that emphasizes the "health and wealth" prosperity gospel. One comes from a traditional Mennonite church. Each one is trying to decide between a new BMW sports sedan and a used Toyota Corolla. The Mennonite man prays a bit, but in his heart he knows that God would want him to have the used Toyota. It just makes more practical sense. The health and wealth guy knows in his heart that God wants to bless him and give him the best. He also prays and asks God's will, but in his heart he is already excited about the BMW. He knows that God wants to bless him and give him the best.

Which man heard the voice of the Lord? Neither. Each one was so convinced that he knew what God wanted that each never laid down his opinions and waited for the Lord to speak. They each assumed that they knew what God wanted because of their religious background. If you want to hear the voice of the Lord, you must quiet the other voices! You must kill the voice of your fleshly desire and the voice of religion. The Lord speaks when you have truly died to your own opinion, when you have placed your desires upon the altar, when you are willing to accept His answer no matter what His answer is.

RUN FROM RELIGION

If you want to be led by the Spirit of God, and become a son of God, it means that the voice of the Holy Spirit must take its rightful place in your life. It means that the voice of the Spirit will carry more weight than the other voices. It means that when you make major decisions, you inquire of the Lord, seeking Him until He speaks.

Many people attempt to hear the Lord, but they are not willing to wait for His answer. The first voice that speaks to them in a convincing manner, they decide is the Lord's. and so they live their life according to the other voices, even as they pretend to be following the Lord.

The Lord will answer when you seek Him, but sometimes that answer takes time. Daniel waited 21 days for the Lord's answer to his questions (Daniel 10:13). The Lord does not always answer immediately. When He isn't speaking, don't pretend that He is speaking! Continue asking, seeking, knocking until you know in your heart what the answer is.

Personally, the major changes of direction in my life have usually been the result of extended times of prayer and fasting. This time of seeking the Lord is not for the purpose of trying to convince the Lord to do what I want. It is a time when I come into alignment with the will of God, laying everything on the altar before Him. I lay down my life and my future. I take time away from people, quieting the voices that can distract me. I wait for Him to speak.

There must come a strong distaste in you for religion. You must absolutely detest the nice words that seem to be from God, but they feel somehow fake. Run from things that look good but which have no life. Refuse to take part in empty religious rituals. Beware of traditions, traditional ways of doing things that are not imbued with power. Hunger for what is alive, for what God is breathing upon. Love His presence, love His anointing. Hate the fake and the substitute.

One of my friends has taught me in this. Katana, in Kenya, is one of the most spiritually hungry people I have ever met. He seeks the Lord with a wholehearted intensity that I have rarely witnessed in my life. He seeks day after day, week after week, with wholehearted worship and prayer. The Lord always answers and speaks with amazing clarity and power.

MEN OF ACTION
It is not those who hear the voice of the Spirit who are the sons of God who bring freedom to the earth. Those who are led by the Spirit are the sons of God. It is not enough to hear. One must also obey.

It is impossible to be a man led by the Holy Spirit without also being a man of action. It is impossible to obey God and follow God without being a man of action.

Many people think of Christianity as being a long list of things that you can't do: don't drink, don't smoke, don't commit sexual immorality. Christianity is not a list of things that you are not allowed to do. True Christianity is an adventure.

The Holy Spirit is moving, and He wants you to move with Him. When you obey the Holy Spirit, He takes you to places you never imagined. When you obey the Holy Spirit, He gives you boldness and courage to do exploits. He also provides amazing creativity to do things in new and better ways.

We live in a world that is ruled and oppressed by the Evil One. We are called to work with God in liberating this fallen earth. We are called to be part of a great battle and a great harvest.

In James 2, we read about the works of faith, and the men of action who do these works.

> What does *it* profit, my brethren, if someone says he has faith but does not have works? Can faith save him? If a brother or sister is naked and destitute of daily food, and one of you says to them, "Depart in peace, be warmed and filled," but you do not give them the things which are needed for the body, what *does it* profit? Thus also faith by itself, if it does not have works, is dead.
>
> But someone will say, "You have faith, and I have works."
>
> Show me your faith without your works, and I will show you my faith by my works. You believe that there is one God. You do well. Even the demons believe—and tremble!
>
> But do you want to know, O foolish man, that faith without works is dead? Was not Abraham our father justified by works when he offered Isaac his son on the altar? Do you see that faith was working together with his works, and by works faith

was made perfect? And the Scripture was fulfilled which says, "Abraham believed God, and it was accounted to him for righteousness." And he was called the friend of God. You see then that a man is justified by works, and not by faith only.

Likewise, was not Rahab the harlot also justified by works when she received the messengers and sent *them* out another way? For as the body without the spirit is dead, so faith without works is dead also (James 2:14-26).

In this Scripture, James tells us that faith without works is dead. When I first read this scripture, I thought that the "works" that James talks about are the feeding and clothing of the poor. I thought this because James compares the man who has faith without works to the man who speaks empty words to a cold and hungry person without actually helping him.

This is not really what James is saying. James gives us two examples of the works that will cause faith to live. The first example is Abraham. James says, "Was not Abraham our father justified by works when he offered Isaac his son on the altar?" The second example is Rahab: "Was not Rahab the harlot also justified by works when she received the messengers and sent them out another way?"

With these two examples, James shows us the kinds of works that must accompany faith. Abraham risked everything when he laid his son Isaac on the altar. Abraham actually believed that even if he sacrificed his son on the altar, God would raise him up again. In Hebrews we are told that Abraham concluded "that God was able to raise him up, even from the dead, from which he also received him in a figurative sense" (Hebrews 11:19).

In other words, it wasn't enough for Abraham to just say that he believed in a God who could raise the dead. Abraham needed to take an action together with his faith. Abraham needed to actually lay his son on the altar, believing that God would do a miracle on his behalf. That is faith! James said, "I will show you my faith by my works." Abraham showed his faith in God by the actions that he took.

Likewise, Rahab risked everything when she decided to put her faith in the God of Israel and rescue the Israelite spies. For years, Rahab heard stories about the God of Israel, who delivered his people from slavery in Egypt, who parted the Red Sea, and performed many miracles on behalf of his people. Now, in Jericho, she discovered the two spies who had been sent to spy out the land.

Obviously, if Rahab were caught helping these enemy spies, she would be killed together with the spies. Rahab decided to risk her life and to put her trust in the God of Israel that she had heard about. She hid the spies from her own countrymen, risking her own life and the life of her family. As she took this action, she proved that she was putting her trust in the God of Israel.

Are you a person of action? If someone looks at the actions you take in life, will they see evidence that you believe? It is not enough for you to quote all the right biblical doctrines. What happens when you are put to the test like Abraham was? Do you take the actions that the Holy Spirit tells you to take? When the Holy Spirit tells you to leave everything and follow Him, do you obey? When the Holy Spirit tells you to give away your possessions, do you do so? When the Holy Spirit tells you to take a step of faith, and declare God's healing for a sick person, do you take the step of faith.?

Another way of saying "faith without works is dead" is to say "faith without action is dead." If you truly believe, faith will be seen in your actions.

THE MEN AND WOMEN OF ACADEMIA
This is why academia is such a toxic and dangerous place. Academic men love to say and write radical things, but they don't usually put their theories into practice. Academic men are not usually men of action.

The scribes were the academic men of Jesus' day. When Jesus was confronted with a scribe who wanted to follow him, Jesus warned the scribe: "Foxes have holes, and birds of the air have nests, but the son of man has no place to lay his head " (Luke 9:58).

With this warning, Jesus confronted the scribe with the reality of his life. Scribes live in academia, a very protected, safe, and secure environment. This scribe had a good position in the religious institution of his day. He didn't need to worry about where his next meal would come from. This is why Jesus warned him that he would have to leave that place of security if he truly desired to follow Jesus.

The true disciples of Christ are not usually found in academia. Jesus did not choose many scholars; nor were many scholars willing to leave their safe and secure places to follow Jesus. Jesus knew what was in the heart of a scholar. He knew which ones were truly radical, men of action, which ones were cowards, and which ones were addicted to the comfort and acclaim of academia.

BECOMING A MAN OF ACTION

Maybe you are not a man of action. Maybe you have a lot of fears. I have some good news for you. When you take steps to obey what the Holy Spirit tells you to do, He will give you courage.

As I have grown older, I have become more aware of my own weaknesses. I don't think I am a very courageous man. I am introverted, feeling awkward and insecure in many social settings. I often struggle with simple tasks. I don't think I am particularly well skilled or well trained in any area.

In spite of my weaknesses, I know that when the Spirit moves in me, I can do many things. With His help, I can move in faith. With his help, I can write books and start schools and churches. I can go into a nation and take actions that have an impact in that nation.

When the Spirit leads me, I can even be courageous. When the Spirit leads me, I can go and speak the Word of God. On several occasions during the past several years, the Lord gave me clear instructions to testify of him publicly in Muslim communities. Sometimes I take my guitar and sing His praises in a Muslim center. Sometimes I preach on the streets. Sometimes I take a group of students and just worship the Lord in the center of an Islamic town for several days. Several times I stood and confronted groups of Muslims who were threatening violence. We do these things under the instruction of the Holy Spirit, and we often experience spiritual breakthroughs as we do them.

This is the inheritance of the sons of God, to move in supernatural power and by supernatural direction. I might be a coward without the Spirit of God, but with the Spirit of God I can take bold action. I know that the Spirit of God will lead me in confrontations with Muslim leaders in different parts of the world. I know that He will lead me to move in miraculous power. I know that the Spirit of God will do amazing things through me if I walk in obedience. Even though I am nothing, I can do all things through Christ who strengthens me. So can you.

Jesus said, **"The wind blows where it wishes, and you hear the sound of it, but cannot tell where it comes from and where it goes. So is everyone who is born of the Spirit"** (John 3:8).

Religious men think they can put God in a box. They use logic and doctrine to try to predict what God will do in any situation. In fact, they do not understand the wind of the Holy Spirit. They do not comprehend what God is doing and why he is doing it. And so they always end up in opposition to the Holy Spirit.

A religious man will always wrongly judge a Spirit-led man. The religious man will assume that the motives of a Spirit-led man are evil. He doesn't really comprehend a man who is not led by religion, by family, by money, or the desire for the praise of man. He doesn't understand someone who actually has a relationship with God. And so he will try to put him in a box, to label him, denigrate him, insult him.

Everything is beautiful in its time (Ecclesiastes 3:11). Religion always tries to lead you to do the wrong thing at the wrong time. When the Holy Spirit is leading you to repent and mourn over your sins, the religious spirit will be telling you that your sins are not serious, that everything has already been forgiven. When it is time to rejoice, the religious spirit will try to bring you into mourning. When it is time to go forward and aggressively preach the gospel, the religious spirit will tell you that it is better for you to stay in your house and pray. When it is time to go deep in prayer and intimacy with the Lord, the religious spirit will try to get you involved in some kind of crusade.

But if you learn to be led by the Holy Spirit, you will discover that you are working with the wind, and not against it. Instead of rowing your boat against the wind, you will discover that the wind is pushing you forward. You will discover that God's grace and presence is upon everything you do, because you are being led by Him.

This is the light yoke, the easy yoke (Matthew 11:30). There is work to be done, but God is with you in the work, helping you carry the yoke that He gives you. When you evangelize, you will discover that God's presence is there. There is an excitement in the air, a great joy. As you talk to people about Jesus, you will have the sense that God is the one breathing upon your conversation, leading you to the right people.

When you worship, you will feel the wind of the Spirit directing your worship. The Holy Spirit will direct the songs that you sing and will give life to those songs. You will discover new songs flowing out of your heart as you sing to the Lord.

And when it is time to repent, your repentance will not be the dead strivings of religion. You will feel the heart of God. You will see your sin through his eyes, and you will mourn because you have hurt His heart. True repentance comes by the Spirit of God, not through the condemnation of religion.

If God is for you, who can be against you? If the Holy Spirit is breathing upon you and your work and helping you in your work, your work will surely succeed.

STARTING OVER
What should you do if the church you are a part of has been hijacked by religion? What should you do if the schools that your children attend have been hijacked? What should your church do if the Mennonite conference it is a part of has been hijacked to such a degree

that it supports sexual perversion in the name of love and the most terrorist-celebrating community in the world in the name of peace? What if your church has been hijacked by a more traditional form of religion, by those who obey a form of religious legalism?

Jesus taught about the hijackers in the parable of the wheat and the tares (Matthew 13: 24-30, 36-43). The tares are sown in the field by the evil one. In their immaturity, they look just like the wheat, just as the cuckoo eggs look like the reed warbler's eggs. If you try to remove the tares at the wrong time, you end up removing the wheat with them. Jesus told his followers to allow the tares to remain until the harvest, when they would be gathered up and burned.

Jesus explained that the field is the world, not the church. In the big picture, it is necessary to let the tares remain in the world. If we try to root out every religious person from the world, we will surely fail. At the same time, Jesus did not instruct us to permit the tares to remain in the church. The New Testament contains many accounts of confrontations with religion. Paul, the apostle, constantly confronted and exposed the religious cuckoo birds that were attempting to hijack the church. Jesus did the same. They refused to allow the tares of religion to be planted inside their communities of faith.

God himself will judge the tares planted in the world, the sons of the Evil One. This judgment takes place at the end of the age, at the time of harvest. The tares will be bundled together, and cast into the fire. At this very moment, a certain bundling is taking place. Groups of tares are uniting together against the Lord and against every biblical standard. They are actually rejecting and casting out anyone who holds onto a biblical standard of righteousness. They are ensuring that the ones in their midst are purely committed to the politically correct view of everything. They have bundled themselves together for judgment, and that judgment is coming.

What should be done in a church where the tares have grown to such a degree that they are suffocating the wheat? What should be done with a nest that has been infested with cuckoo chicks? Should you stay committed to a church in which the leaders have been hijacked?

Should a church stay committed to a denomination that has been hijacked and is openly rejecting biblical Christianity?

LEARNING FROM THE REED WARBLER

When the eggs of the cuckoo are laid in the reed warbler's nest, some reed warblers are able to stop the hijack attempt. Some reed warblers have a high level of discernment, and they are able to eject the egg of the cuckoo bird so that they can raise their own offspring instead of allowing the cuckoo chick to hijack the nest, kill their offspring, and monopolize the life and efforts of the parents. Studies have shown that about 12 percent of reed warblers are able to identify and cast out the eggs of the cuckoo bird.[16]

In other cases, the reed warblers know something has gone wrong, but they are unable to identify the cuckoo eggs to cast out of the nest. In these cases, the reed warbler abandons its nest and builds a new nest. This takes place about 20 percent of the time. The rest of the time, about two-thirds of the time, the reed warblers raise the cuckoo chick as if it were their own after it has killed their own offspring.

It is very, very difficult to save a church that has been hijacked. When the followers of the religion of political correctness grab a church or a denomination, they do not easily let go. They think that church belongs to them. They think the ones who are trying to obey the Spirit of God and the Word of God are the imposters. They have the spirit of Cain, the spirit of Ishmael, and they think that they are the rightful heir of the church.

Many people spend their lives hoping to change a church that has been hijacked. These people can certainly be a blessing to individuals in the church and can minister to people who are dying under the oppression of religion. Unfortunately, the church itself is very rarely ever rescued from the hijackers. The leadership rarely changes its position.

---

[16] Moskát, C.; Honza, M. (2002). "European Cuckoo Cuculus canorus parasitism and host's rejection behaviour in a heavily parasitized Great Reed Warbler Acrocephalus arundinaceus population"

When you are trapped in a system that is infested with religion, it is often better to leave that system and start over. You can either spend your life like the majority of reed warblers whose nests have been hijacked, feeding a cuckoo chick, or you can start over, build a new nest, and lay fresh eggs. Starting over is a better solution than spending your life serving religion! Building a new nest is a better solution than spending the rest of your life trying to satisfy an ugly, fat cuckoo chick!

There are many people trapped in religious systems that simply need to start over. They must leave that religious system. If they do not leave, their lives will be wasted. Any new life that comes from them will quickly be killed by the cuckoo birds. If they lead someone to the Lord, the religious people in their midst will quickly criticize and destroy the new convert. The cuckoo chicks will kill any chicks that are not like themselves.

Some have been called by God to minister within hijacked churches and institutions. This is a temporary calling. These people will not save the church or the institution, but God will use them to touch the lives of hurting individuals. But when the time of judgment comes, even those who were called to work for a time in hijacked institutions need to leave those institutions. The tares will be bundled together and thrown into the fire.

Starting over is often the best option for those who are connected to a hijacked religious institution. It is usually better to go back to the beginning. Start a fellowship that meets in your home. Worship the Lord together and preach the gospel. Let the religious have their institution. It will soon wither and die. Focus on new life. Make sure that you actually know the Lord and His voice and not just the voice of religion. Focus on reaching your neighborhood with the gospel. Find like-minded people who love the ministry and power and leading of the Holy Spirit. Find likeminded people who are committed to the authority of the Word of God. Work with them, seek the Lord with them, and obey His instructions. Take action.

The church that is alive, that has not been hijacked, will always have new life. Those who are following the Spirit will have the fruit of the Spirit.

It is usually better to simply start over. I watched my father minister for many years in religious systems. He was a pastor and a bishop in the Mennonite church. It was very difficult for my father to step down as a bishop in the Mennonite church. It was even more difficult for him to say goodbye to his beloved denomination. But as he did so, life began to flow in new ways. Today my father is pastor of a growing church that is reaching many in its community.

This doesn't mean that everyone who has a position in the Mennonite church should follow the example of my father. It is important to obey the Spirit of God. If you have a position, you need to be sure that it is one given to you by the Holy Spirit. My father didn't step out of his position because of bad feelings against the church or anyone in it. It was the Spirit of God that instructed him to leave.

One way to tell whether or not a church has been hijacked is by the new life, the new conversions in that church. In a church controlled by religion, there are no new converts. The cuckoo chicks ensure that new believers cannot find their place in a hijacked church. This is true in liberal churches and conservative ones. When a church is hijacked by any form of religion, there are very few people who find Christ there. The only growth that takes place is either transfer growth from other churches or numerical growth from members having large families.

If you are looking for a church, look for one that is actually reaching the lost with the gospel. Look for a church where people are encountering Jesus, where new believers are being born, raised and discipled. If there are no new believers, something is wrong. The church has probably been hijacked.

CAN A RELIGIOUS MAN BE SAVED?

Starting over is also necessary for individuals who are bound by religion. A very religious man, a Pharisee, came to Jesus to question him about the kingdom of God. Jesus said to that man, **"Most assuredly, I say to you, unless one is born again, he cannot see the kingdom of God"** (John 3:3).

What does it mean to be born again? It means to go back to the very beginning and start over. This religious Pharisee probably thought that his training and religious knowledge had value. He probably wanted to add whatever Jesus could give him to what he already had. But that is not how the kingdom works.

The religious training of that Pharisee was worse than useless. The religion of the Pharisees did not lead people to God. The religious system of the Pharisees inspired them to oppose and attack God in the flesh.

If you are religious, you need to start over. Your education will not save you. Your religious opinions are not God's opinions. The kingdom you know about is not the kingdom of heaven.

A religious man usually receives something from the religious system that he serves-- position, money, and the praise of man. Jesus spoke about the positions of honor and the praise of man that the Pharisees received from their religion: **"Everything they do is done for people to see...they love the place of honor at banquets and the most important seats in the synagogues; they love to be greeted with respect in the marketplaces and to be called 'Rabbi' by others"** (Matthew 23:6-7). He said to them, **"How can you believe since you accept glory from one another but do not seek the glory that comes from the only God?"** (John 5:44)

At the top of the religious systems are persons who make their living from religion. They do not want to see the system shaken because the system provides their income. The Pharisees tried to protect their system of religion from threats such as Jesus, who could damage their finances.

Religious persons need to start over. For those who are benefiting from the religious system, they need to give up those benefits. It would be far better for a bishop who is bound by religion to quit his religious job and work at McDonalds. At McDonalds all his religious pretention would be cast aside. At McDonalds, he could start over as a child at the very beginning.

This is necessary when someone is saved out of religion. In a Muslim setting, the persecution that new believers face causes religious men to start over from the beginning. I recently helped baptize Abdullah (not his real name), one of the leading imams in East Africa. For many years Abdullah followed his religion and opposed the Christian faith. His son had an encounter with the Lord and became a preacher. We worked with his son from time to time. The son asked us to pray for his father. Every time he visited his father, his father would chase him from the home.

We didn't realize it, but God was busy with Abdullah. Abdullah received dreams from God in which he saw that the path he was on was leading him to destruction. He heard a voice telling him to follow the path of his son. After receiving these dreams, the Muslim leaders of Abdullah's city came to him and asked him to be their leader. Abdullah responded, "I cannot accept this offer. I have decided to follow a different path." He decided to follow his son in following Christ.

And so Abdullah, the great imam, lost everything he had known before. He lost his religious position. His house was burned to the ground, and he fled for his life. We baptized him in the Indian Ocean and helped him into hiding.

Abdullah needed to start over, from the beginning. The knowledge of God that he gained through his religion was a bondage. He lost everything, and he gained eternal life.

A religious man can be saved and become a true man of God, but it is not an easy path. A religious man usually wants to hold on to his position, and his good works. He holds on to his righteousness that he has attained through his religious efforts. He becomes indignant at the foolishness of small children who know God better than he does. He becomes indignant when God uses the foolish things of this world to confound the wise. He takes people lightly, not seeing the true value or calling. He doesn't realize that those new believers, those untrained people, know more about God's life and power than he does. He needs to go to the back of the line and be born again.

As a great shaking takes place in the Mennonite Church, it is necessary to know that God is raising up new leaders. Those who rose up in the religious systems of men are disqualified from leading the way into the kingdom. God will lift up simple men, often untrained in any religious institution, who know His voice and obey Him completely.

A MOVEMENT AMONG THE MENNONITES

I believe that God will do a wonderful work among the Mennonites, among those who come from a Mennonite background. I believe that He will fulfill His good plans and purposes for the Mennonite church. Mennonites will be freed from the power of religion. They will become radical preachers of the gospel of peace. They will go into the nations, declaring and demonstrating the kingdom of heaven.

I do not have faith in the Mennonite organizations and religious institutions. I believe that many of them have been hijacked by religion. I do not believe that God will use them to fulfill His promises for the Mennonite church.

There is something good in the Anabaptist heritage. There was a radical reformation that took place during the early days of the Anabaptists. This reformation was intended to transform Europe. I believe that many who come from a Mennonite background are called to tap into this heritage and walk in the paths of their forefathers. They are called to overcome by the blood of the Lamb, by the word of their testimony, and they will not love their lives to the death. This was the message of my first book for the Mennonites: *There is a Way Back*. I still believe in that message.

You do not need to be called a Mennonite to walk out the purpose for the Mennonites. God is bringing forth a movement of the Holy Spirit out of the Anabaptist root system. It is not necessary that those who are part of this movement be connected to the Mennonite religious institutions. It might be better if they are not.

10 THE SPIRITUAL HIJACKING OF MOTHER TERESA

Mother Teresa was born August 26, 1910, in the Macedonian town of Skopje. Her name was Agnes Gonxhe Bojaxhiu, daughter of Nkolle and Dranafile Bojaxhiu. As a young girl Agnes showed a deep love for religion. She was especially fascinated by the stories of Roman Catholic missionaries to India.

The Bojaxhiu family was a very religious family. They made yearly pilgrimage to a shrine of the Virgin Mary. They tried to live out the golden rule, "Do unto others as you would have them do unto you." When violence swept across the region, the family opened up their home to the destitute. Those who lost homes, families and livelihoods often joined the family for dinner.

Agnes loved God. From the age of five and a half years, when she took her first communion, she felt a desire to reach souls for Jesus Christ. At the age of 12, during one of her family's pilgrimages to the shrine of Mary, she felt called to devote her life to God's work.

As time went on, the calling grew inside her. At the age of 18, Agnes left her home in Albania to join the Sisters of Loreto in Dublin, Ireland. There she studied English and prepared to become a missionary. On

December 1, 1928, Agnes boarded a boat for India, and never looked back.

In India, Agnes became a novitiate at a convent in Darjeeling, in the foothills of the Himalayas. There she studied the Bengali language and prepared to take her vows as a nun. On May 24, 1931, she had her first profession of vows and became a full member of the sisters of Loreto. She chose to change her name to Teresa, in honor of St Therese de Lisieux, patron saint of missionaries.

After becoming a nun, Sister Teresa moved to the city of Calcutta, where the sisters of Loreto had a large compound. Within their walls were several schools enrolling about 500 students. For the most part, the nuns of Saint Loreto stayed inside their compound, rarely venturing out into the city.

In 1935, Sister Teresa started teaching in a school, St Teresa's, that was located outside the walls of the compound. This required her to take daily walks through Calcutta. As she did so, she saw the multitudes of homeless on the streets of Calcutta, and her heart went out to them.

In 1946, after 18 years working as a nun, Mother Teresa had a supernatural experience as she rode on a train to a retreat in the Himalayas. In the encounter, she felt a voice instructing her to begin a mission to the poorest of the poor. She received a vision to start a new religious community that would go outside the walls of the convent and onto the streets of Calcutta. This religious community would not start schools to teach the children of middle class Indians as the Sisters of Loreto had done. This religious community would work with the poorest of the poor in the streets of Calcutta.

During the following months, Mother Teresa had several similar encounters with what she called "the voice." Mother Teresa was convinced that this voice was the voice of Christ. This voice instructed her about the new ministry that she would start. In particular, she received three visions. This is her account:

1) I saw a very big crowd—all kinds of people—very poor and children were there also. They all had their hands lifted towards

me—standing in their midst. They called out "Come, come, save us—bring us to Jesus."

2) Again that great crowd—I could see great sorrow and suffering in their faces—I was kneeling near Our Lady, who was facing them.—I did not see her face but I heard her say "Take care of them—they are mine.—Bring them to Jesus—carry Jesus to them.—Fear not. Teach them to say the Rosary—the family Rosary and all will be well.—Fear not—Jesus and I will be with you and your children."

3) The same great crowd—they were covered in darkness. Yet I could see them. Our Lord on the Cross. Our Lady at a little distance from the Cross—and myself as a little child in front of her. Her left hand was on my left shoulder—and her right hand was holding my right arm. We were both facing the Cross. Our Lord said—"I have asked you. They have asked you and she, My Mother has asked you. Will you refuse to do this for Me—to take care of them, to bring them to Me?" (Kolodiejchuk p. 98)

The voice pressured Teresa to accept the call:

Wilt thou refuse? When there was a question of thy soul I did not think of Myself but gave Myself freely for thee on the Cross and now what about thee? Wilt thou refuse? I want Indian nuns victims of My love, who would be Mary and Martha, who would be so very united to Me as to radiate My love on souls. I want free nuns covered with My poverty of the Cross. I want obedient nuns covered with My obedience on the Cross. I want full of love nuns covered with My Charity of the Cross. Wilt thou refuse to do this for Me?

You have become My Spouse for My love—you have come to India for Me. The thirst you had for souls brought you so far. Are you afraid now to take one more step for your Spouse—for Me—for souls? Is your generosity grown cold? Am I a second to you? You did not die for souls—that is why you don't care what happens to them. Your heart was never drowned in sorrow as was My Mother's. We both gave our all for souls—and you? You are afraid, that you will lose your vocation—you will become a secular—you will be wanting in perseverance. No—your vocation is to love and suffer and save souls and by taking the step you will fulfill My Heart's desire for you. (Kolodiejchuk p. 95-96)

My little one—come—come—carry Me into the holes of the poor. Come be My light. I cannot go alone—they don't know Me—so they don't want Me. You come—go amongst them, carry Me with you into them. How I long to enter their holes—their dark unhappy homes. Come be their victim. In your immolation—in your love for Me—they will see Me, know Me, want Me. Offer more sacrifices—smile more tenderly, pray more fervently and all the difficulties will disappear.

You are afraid. How your fear hurts Me. Fear not. It is I who am asking you to do this for Me. Fear not. Even if the whole world is against you, laughs at you, your companions and Superiors look down on you, fear not—it is I in you, with you, for you. You will suffer—suffer very much—but remember I am with you. Even if the whole world rejects you—remember you are My own—and I am yours only. Fear not. It is I. Only obey—obey very cheerfully and promptly and without any questions—just only obey. I shall never leave you—if you obey. (Kolodiejchuk p. 98)

How could Mother Teresa respond? What choice did she have? Mary pleaded with her to accept the task. Jesus pleaded with her to accept the task. And the people pleaded with her.

The voice that pleaded with her carried much weight with her. Four years earlier, in April 1942, Teresa made a solemn vow to God. Mother Teresa wrote concerning this vow, "I made a vow to God, binding under pain of mortal sin, to give to God anything He may ask, 'Not to refuse Him anything.'" (Kolodiejchuk p. 27)

A mortal sin according to Roman Catholic theology is a sin which is a grave violation of God's law. The person who commits a mortal sin is excluded from Christ's kingdom and condemned to hell unless he repents and receives forgiveness.

Teresa had a strong desire to be completely obedient to the Lord. As she accepted the call of the voice, she wrote to her overseers, "... I have been longing to be all for Jesus and to make other souls—

especially Indian, come and love Him fervently—to identify myself with Indian girls completely, and so love Him as He has never been loved before." (Kolodiejchuk p. 46)

For a period of six months, Teresa listened to the voice. The voice convinced her that she needed to leave the sheltered walls of the convent and the schools and go to the streets. The voice convinced her to start a religious community that would help the poorest of the poor.

As the voice pressured Teresa, Teresa pressured her religious overseers to permit her to start her new religious community. On October 7, 1950, Pope Pius XI himself gave his approval, and the Society of the Missionaries of Charity was begun in the archdiocese of Calcutta.

Mother Teresa wrote down her plans and the primary purpose of her new order, that eventually formed its constitution. She wrote:

> The general aim of the Missionaries of Charity is to satiate the thirst of Jesus Christ on the Cross for love and souls by the Sisters, [through] absolute poverty, angelic chastity, cheerful obedience. The Particular End is to carry Christ into the homes and streets of the slums, [among] the sick, dying, the beggars and the little street children. The sick will be nursed as far as possible in their poor homes. The little children will have a school in the slums. The beggars will be sought and visited in their holes outside the town or on the streets. To be able to do all these—the Sisters must learn first to live real interior lives of close union with God—and seek and see Him in all they do for the poor. There will be no difference amongst the Sisters—they must all learn farming, cooking, nursing and a little teaching—and be ready always to do any of these works if obedience requires. (Kolodiejchuk appendix A)

The new religious order took off. The first year, there were 13 sisters, working on the streets of Calcutta. They provided basic schooling for the poor children of Calcutta. They visited the poor and sick, and did what they could.

On October 7, 1950, Teresa received Vatican permission for the diocesan congregation which would become the Missionaries of Charity. In her words, it would care for "the hungry, the naked, the homeless, the crippled, the blind, the lepers, all those people who feel unwanted, unloved, uncared for throughout society, people that have become a burden to the society and are shunned by everyone." By 1997 the 13-member Calcutta congregation had grown to more than 4,000 sisters who managed orphanages, AIDS hospices and charity centers worldwide, caring for refugees, the blind, disabled, aged, alcoholics, the poor and homeless and victims of floods, epidemics and famine.

Mother Teresa became famous for her great work. She received award after award. She raised hundreds of millions of dollars for her work among the poor.

With such a dramatic calling and such dramatic results, there would seem to be little doubt that Mother Teresa knew the Lord and that He blessed her work. Unfortunately, the reality is quite different.

After Mother Teresa's death, her private diaries were released to the public. They revealed a hidden part of Mother Teresa's life that shocked the public. Many of these private writings were compiled in Brian Kolodiejchuk's book *Come be My Light*, from which I draw the following quotations.

Here is one rather typical entry, from September 3, 1959:

> "My own Jesus, From my childhood you have called me and kept me for Your own—and now when we both have taken the same road—now Jesus—I go the wrong way.
>
> They say people in hell suffer eternal pain because of the loss of God—they would go through all that suffering if they had just a little hope of possessing God. In my soul I feel just that terrible pain of loss—of God not wanting me—of God not being God— of God not really existing (Jesus, please forgive my blasphemies— I have been told to write everything). That darkness that surrounds me on all sides—I can't lift my soul to God—no light or inspiration enters my soul. I speak of love for souls—of tender

love for God—words pass through my words [sic, lips]—and I long with a deep longing to believe in them.—What do I labour for? If there be no God—there can be no soul. If there is no soul then Jesus—You also are not true.—Heaven, what emptiness— not a single thought of Heaven enters my mind—for there is no hope. I am afraid to write all those terrible things that pass in my soul. They must hurt You. In my heart there is no faith—no love—no trust—there is so much pain—the pain of longing, the pain of not being wanted. I want God with all the powers of my soul—and yet there between us—there is terrible separation. I don't pray any longer—I utter words of community prayers—and try my utmost to get out of every word the sweetness it has to give. But my prayer of union is not there any longer.—I no longer pray. My soul is not one with You—and yet when alone in the streets— I talk to You for hours—of my longing for You. How intimate are those words—and yet so empty, for they leave me far from You.— The work holds no joy, no attraction, no zeal. I remember, I told Mother Provincial, that I was leaving Loreto—for souls— for a single soul—and she could not understand my words. I do my best. I spend myself—but I am more than convinced that the work is not mine. I do not doubt that it was You who called me, with so much love and force. It was You—I know. That is why the work is Yours and it is You even now—but I have no faith— I don't believe. (Kolodiejchuk p. 191)

For fifty years, Mother Teresa's letters and diary entries reveal a deeply tormented soul. They reveal the heart of someone who is deeply convinced that God has abandoned her, if, indeed, there is a God. They reveal a deep sense of rejection, discouragement and depression, with almost no ray of light penetrating the darkness.

Mother Teresa looked for help, until she became so depressed that she began to accept her condition. When the sisters of her order went on spiritual retreats, she hoped for relief from her suffering. And yet in retreat after retreat, she didn't find what she was looking for.

In one retreat in 1959, the participants were asked to honestly answer some questions regarding their spiritual condition. Here are a few questions together with Teresa's answers from that retreat:

Do I really try to praise, reverence and serve God?
Answer: I want but I don't.
Do I put this into daily practice? In ALL my actions?
Answer: No. Except for the first offering to the S.H. [Sacred Heart]
in the morning—the rest of the day is like a stone. Yet my heart is all
and only His—my mind & will are fixed on Him—the whole time.
Do I value the salvation of my soul?
Answer: I don't believe I have a soul. There is nothing in me.
Am I working in earnest for the salvation of the souls of others?
Answer: There was a burning zeal in my soul for souls from
childhood until I said "yes" to God & then all is gone. Now I don't
believe.... (Kolodiejchuk appendix B)

Mother Teresa repeatedly testified that from the moment she said
"yes" to the voice and started the Missionaries of charity, she entered
a time of deep spiritual darkness and depression.

Teresa turned to various spiritual advisors and overseers as she tried
to understand what had gone wrong. One of these advisers was
Father Neuner. Father Neuner and others tried to answer Teresa's
questions by having her read teachings on the *Dark night of the Soul* by
St. John of the Cross. St. John talked about periods of desperation
and darkness in one's life that eventually led to unity with God.

Unfortunately, for Teresa, the night never turned to day. The darkness
and depression in her life continued day after day, year after year.
Teresa's spiritual advisers proved to be quite adept at finding religious
explanations for her miserable experiences.

Father Neuner and others decided that Teresa was experiencing the
suffering of Jesus on the cross. They decided that her suffering was
actually a gift from God, that Jesus was allowing her to share in his
own experience at the cross.

In her desperate spiritual condition, Mother Teresa finally came into
agreement with her advisers. She decided that indeed, the deep
darkness and discouragement that surrounded her must be God's gift.

She declared that she had come to love the darkness because it was given to her from God.

In a letter to Father Neuner in 1961, she wrote:
> For the first time in this 11 years—I have come to love the darkness—for I believe now that it is a part a very, very small part of Jesus' darkness & pain on earth. You have taught me to accept it [as] a "spiritual side of 'your work,'" as you wrote (Kolodiejchuk p. 208).

She became convinced that as she walked in darkness, it would help her to reach people who were in darkness. She thought that even if she became a saint, she wouldn't reside in heaven. She thought she would continue to walk in darkness so that she could help those who were trapped in darkness on earth. She writes: "If I ever become a Saint—I will surely be one of 'darkness.' I will continually be absent from Heaven—to light the light of those in darkness on earth." (Kolodiejchuk p.229)

The Bible clearly teaches that the rivers of life flow from the heart. If the heart is not in a good condition, nothing good will come from the heart. If your heart is not filled with the love and presence of God, you really have nothing to give anyone.

Mother Teresa became famous. The rich and powerful honored her with the highest honors that men can give. Teresa won the Nobel Peace prize in 1979. She received a long list of other awards from governments and humanitarian associations. Everywhere she went she was honored and revered as a living saint. She was considered to be shoo-in for sainthood after death.

Even if Mother Teresa's personal life was off track, it seemed like her ministry was experiencing amazing success. Thousands of people worked in her organizations in many nations to help the poor.

And yet, as successful as Teresa's life and ministry seemed to be, there were some warning signs. Those who got an up-close look at the ministry often went away with the impression that something was wrong. Yes, Teresa and the sisters made great sacrifices as they lived their lives in the slums of large cities. And yet…why were the conditions in the homes so spartan and harsh?

Here are several testimonies from these homes compiled by Christopher Hitchens in his 1995 book *The Missionary Position*. Mary Loudon, a volunteer in Calcutta wrote the following:

> My initial impression was of all the photographs and footage I've ever seen of Belsen and places like that, because all the patients had shaved heads. No chairs anywhere, there were just these stretcher beds. They're like First World War stretcher beds. There's no garden, no yard even. No nothing. And I thought what is this? This is two rooms with fifty to sixty men in one, fifty to sixty women in another. They're dying. They're not being given a great deal of medical care. They're not being given painkillers really beyond aspirin and maybe if you're lucky some Brufen or something, for the sort of pain that goes with terminal cancer and the things they were dying of…

> They didn't have enough drips. The needles they used and re-used over and over and over and you would see some of the nuns rinsing needles under the cold water tap. And I asked one of them why she was doing it and she said: "Well to clean it." And I said, "Yes, but why are you not sterilizing it; why are you not boiling water and sterilizing your needles?" She said: "There's no point. There's no time."

> The first day I was there when I'd finished working in the women's ward I went and waited on the edge of the men's ward for my boyfriend, who was looking after a boy of fifteen who was dying, and an American doctor told me that she had been trying to treat this boy. And that he had a really relatively simple kidney complaint that had simply got worse and worse and worse because he hadn't had antibiotics. And he actually needed an operation. I don't recall what the problem was, but she did tell me. And she was so angry, but also very resigned which so many people become in that situation. And she said, "Well, they won't take him to hospital." And I said: "Why? All you have to do is get a cab. Take him to the nearest hospital, demand that he has treatment. Get him an operation." She said: "They don't do it. They won't do it. If they

do it for one, they do it for everybody." And I thought—but this kid is fifteen.[17]

Susan Shields worked for nine and a half years as a member of the Sisters of Charity. She witnessed many things during that time. In San Francisco, the sisters were given a convent. This convent was perfectly set up for a religious institution. Unfortunately, it wasn't "good" enough for the Sisters of Charity:

> The sisters lost no time in disposing of the unwanted furnishing. They removed the benches from the chapel and pulled up all the carpeting in the rooms and hallways. They pushed thick mattresses out the windows and removed all the sofas, chairs and curtains from the premises. People from the neighborhood stood on the sidewalk and watched in amazement... The heat remained off all winter in this exceedingly damp house. Several sisters got TB during the time I lived there.[18]

Why did so many people experience such a harshness, such a coldness in their dealings with the Sisters of Charity? These Sisters put smiles on their faces and gave religious answers to every question. And yet, something was wrong.

Mother Teresa pretended to have the love of God. She spoke constantly about the love of God. And yet her private communications repeatedly witnessed that she did not know the love of God. She did not feel love for God, and she did not feel that God loved her. And so she pasted on a religious, smiling face, day after day, and pretended to know the love of God.

In reality, Mother Teresa was suffering. With the help of her spiritual advisers, she decided that her suffering was a gift from God, and she needed to accept it. Inevitably, this twisted view of God and his gifts affected the way she treated others. Once, in an address, Mother Teresa gave the testimony of a man who was suffering under intense

---

[17]*Hitchens, Christopher (1995). The Missionary Position: Mother Teresa in Theory and Practice. London:*, pp 39-41
[18] *Hitchens, p. 45*

pain from cancer.   Mother Teresa said to the man, "You are suffering like Christ on the cross. So Jesus must be kissing you."   The man replied, "Then please tell him to stop kissing me!" [19]

Quite simply, Mother Teresa believed that her suffering came from God, and she believed that the suffering and sickness of the poor also came from God. The answer to their problems was not really to alleviate their suffering. The real answer was to bring them to a place where they could thank God for their sickness, their suffering, and their problems. In the 1990's she wrote:

> I think it is very beautiful for the poor to accept their lot, to share it with the passion of Christ. I think the world is being much helped by the suffering of the poor people. [20]

Inevitably, this twisted, perverted view of suffering and sickness turned many people off. People can instinctively feel when words are fake and religious. They also know when someone actually loves them and is speaking truth from the heart.

Jesus said, **"The enemy comes to steal, to kill, and destroy. I have come that you may have life, and have it more abundantly."** (John 10:10) Jesus healed the sick. He never told them to thank God for their sickness!

Religion seems so good and spiritual. Mother Teresa seemed to be the most spiritual person on this planet. And yet, the reality of her life was pitiful.

SMILING THROUGH IT ALL...

Mother Teresa writes: "Sometimes the pain is so great that I feel as if everything will break. The smile is a big cloak which covers a multitude of pains. Pray for me, please. Yours in Jesus, M. Teresa, M.C.." (Kolodiejchuk p. 176)

---

[19] *Address to National Prayer Breakfast, (3 February, 1994)*
[20] *Hitchens. p. 82.*

Mother Teresa's inner condition was rarely seen by outsiders. She became very skilled at placing a smile on her face as she performed her religious duties around the world. People who knew her were always impressed by her religious devotion. She said her prayers with great fervency and prayed the rosary. Yet in her private letters she testified repeatedly that her heart was like ice.

Jesus constantly exposed, confronted, and condemned the religious. He refused to allow them to pretend that they were the sons of God. He did this because he loved them and wanted to reveal the sad reality of their situation so that they might leave their religion and become His followers. He did this so that nobody would be deceived into thinking that the religious knew anything about the path of life.

HIJACKED BY RELIGION

How did Mother Teresa arrive in this condition? From her childhood, Mother Teresa was saturated in religion. Her family went on yearly pilgrimages to worship at the shrine of the Black Madonna of Vitina-Letnice. When Mary's call to ministry came, it was not only Jesus who called her into ministry. Jesus and Mary met with her and asked her to begin her ministry. When she obeyed this call, she entered into deep bondage and depression.

The Bible teaches us that you become the slave of the one whom you obey (Romans 6:16). If you obey a religious spirit, it doesn't matter if you think you are obeying God. It doesn't matter how big a price you pay. You will become the slave of that spirit. You will enter into a deep spiritual bondage.

This bondage can be seen in Teresa's life as she began her ministry. In the Roman Catholic Church, the religious spirit works in certain ways. Perhaps one of the greatest deceptions in Roman Catholicism is found in the way that mortals take the place of God. The authority of mere man is lifted too high, to the point that a person can replace God.

According to Roman Catholic theology, the blood of Jesus Christ cleanses us from original sin, the sin of Adam. However, in order to be forgiven for daily sin, one must go through a priest. For daily, personal sins to be forgiven, one must go to Mass. Only a priest can pray for a piece of bread and turn that bread into the actual body of Jesus Christ. Only a priest can give you that bread so that your personal sins can be forgiven. In practical terms this means that everyone must go through a priest to have forgiveness of sins.

Roman Catholics believe in transubstantiation, that the wine and bread are literally transformed into the body and blood of Jesus Christ. Mother Teresa believed that when a priest came and performed Mass for her new religious society that then Jesus would be present among them. Her faith in this religious ritual is striking. Mother Teresa was overjoyed when she received the news that the archbishop had given his permission for Mass to be held for the first time in the Sisters of Charity chapel. She wrote to the archbishop about the Mass: "Soon Our Lord will be with us.—Everything will be easy then—He will be there personally." (Kolodiejchuk p.139)

The authority of man is elevated very high in Roman Catholicism. Mother Teresa received her religious training from the Sisters of Loreto. The constitution of this organization encouraged a nun to be perfectly obedient to the will and judgment of her superior. As a fervent Loreto Sister, Mother Teresa believed that her religious superiors took the place of Christ, and that as she submitted to their commands, she was submitting to Christ Himself.

When Mother Teresa began the Sisters of Charity, she brought this same understanding of spiritual authority into her new organization. These are some of the rules for the Sisters of Charity that Mother Teresa wrote down as she started the organization in 1947:

> 30. Cheerful Obedience – By this vow the Sister binds herself to obey the lawful Superior – in things which are connected with the life of the Missionaries of Charity
>
> 31. The Sisters will obey cheerfully, promptly, blindly, and simply. They should remember that it is not her or she whom they obey, but He, Jesus Christ, for whose sake and whom they obey in all (Kolokiejchuk Appendix A)

When Mother Teresa sought permission to start the Sisters of Charity, she ensured those who were in authority over her that she would obey them completely. In fact, the same "voice" that instructed her to begin the Sisters of Charity also spoke to her about her spiritual father, Father van Exem, and told her to obey him completely.

This is what the voice said to her:

> People think you were sent here to teach, and you do well and doing the work with the whole of your heart, but this was not the aim of My Heart—I brought you here to be under the immediate care of your spiritual father who will train you in the ways of My love and so prepare you to do My will. Trust him completely and without any fear. Obey him in every detail, you shall not be deceived if you obey for he belongs to Me completely.—I shall let you know My will through him. (Kolokiejchuk p. 81)

Religious persons usually presume an authority that is much greater than the authority that God has actually given them. All authority has limits. Your pastor might have a certain authority given to him by God, but that authority has limits. When he exceeds his authority, it is very necessary to disobey him. He is not God.

Likewise, every human authority has limits. When a president goes beyond his constitutional authority and becomes a dictator, he should be disobeyed. If he isn't, he will oppress the nation. A husband who goes beyond his God-given authority and begins to abuse his wife should be disobeyed. Authority comes from God, but authority has limits.

When religious leaders try to become the "priests" of the ones that they are leading, they have gone too far. A pastor carries a God-given authority to lead his congregation, but he is not the "priest' of his congregation. The people in his congregation do not need to go through that pastor to get to God. They do not need him to perform special rituals for their sins to be forgiven. Every believer is a priest. Every believer can go straight to the Father through the blood of Jesus Christ. Every believer can have his sins forgiven as he/she repents and puts trust in the blood of Jesus Christ that cleanses us from all sin.

THE WORSHIP OF PERSONS

Not only are living persons lifted very high in Catholicism but also dead men and women. Roman Catholics literally pray to the saints, who they believe will help them in their problems and make intercession for them to God.

Mary is exalted most of all. It was Mary and Jesus who called Mother Teresa to her ministry in the slums, and Teresa exalted Mary all the days of her life. Mother Teresa was deeply influenced by the teachings of Saint Louis de Montfort who taught people to surrender themselves as slaves to Mary, and to Jesus through Mary, and to perform all actions "with Mary, in Mary, through Mary, and for Mary.

Mother Teresa wrote to the archbishop about the important place that Mary had in her ministry:

> We are taught to love and say the Rosary with great devotion; let us be very faithful to this our first love—for it will bring us closer to our Heavenly Mother. Our rule asks of us never to go to the slums without first having recited the Mother's praises; that is why we have to say the Rosary in the streets & dark holes of the slums. Cling to the Rosary as the creeper clings to the tree—for without Our Lady we cannot stand (Kolokiejchuk p. 141).

Teresa wrote on another occasion to the archbishop, "I want to become a real slave of Our Lady – to drink only from His chalice of pain and to give Mother Church real saints." (Kolokiejchuk p. 141)

WHOM DID TERESA OBEY?

Whom did Teresa really obey? Mother Teresa talked continually about her love for Christ and her desire to obey Christ. In 1942 she committed herself to never refuse the voice of Christ anything. Yet whom was she really obeying?

Romans 6:16 says, **"Do you not know that when you continually offer yourselves to someone to do his will, you are the slaves of the one whom you obey, either [slaves] of sin, which leads to**

death, or of obedience, which leads to righteousness (right standing with God)? "

Mother Teresa was a slave to religion. The Bible teaches us that you become the slave of the one that you obey. If Mother Teresa listened to the spirit of religion instead of the Holy Spirit, she became a child of religion. She became a slave of religion.

It is very important that you know which voice you are listening to. Mother Teresa committed herself to completely obey whatever Christ asked her to do. When the voice spoke to her and told her to start her ministry, she was convinced that the voice was Christ.

Would Christ really come with Mary and ask someone to start a ministry? Mother Teresa received three visions, one in which Christ asked her to start the ministry, one in which Mary asked her to start her ministry, and one in which the people asked her to start the ministry.

When Mary appeared to Mother Teresa, Mary said, "Fear not. Teach them to say the Rosary—the family Rosary and all will be well. Fear not—Jesus and I will be with you and your children." This was certainly a dramatic experience for Teresa. But did this experience actually come from God? Would God actually speak to someone through Mary and tell them that they should teach poor people to say the rosary?

If we look honestly at what took place, the answer becomes very clear. All was not well when Teresa obeyed the voices. Teresa went into deep depression and came under the bondage of religion as she obeyed the voices. Quite simply, Teresa's life was hijacked by the spirit of religion. Teresa spent her life thinking that she was serving the living Christ while in fact she served the cuckoo birds of religion.

Religion performs many good works, but the works are not the kingdom of heaven. The works appear impressive to men, but they are not the supernatural works of the kingdom. They are the imitation works of religion.

Mother Teresa's great desire was to win souls for Christ. She interpreted Jesus' words at the Cross, "I thirst," as being a thirst for souls and the love of humanity. She wanted to be the one to bring souls to Jesus.

But how can someone who does not actually know Christ bring Christ to anyone? Did the suffering poor in Calcutta actually meet Jesus when they came to the hospices of the Sisters of Charity? The sisters of Charity were taught to secretly evangelize those who were dying. They asked them if they wanted a ticket to heaven. Then they dipped their finger in water and made the sign of the cross on their foreheads, as a kind of baptism. Do you think anyone was actually saved in this way?

Mother Teresa put great faith in the religious rituals of the Catholic Church. She really believed that when the priest prayed for the bread, it became Christ. She put her faith in the leaders of the Catholic church, and in the rituals of the Catholic church. She believed in these things.

But did she actually believe in Jesus? Did she know Jesus? The emptiness and barrenness of her heart would indicate that she did not. How is it possible to know Jesus and not to know His joy? How is it possible to actually know Jesus and not to be changed by His love?

The presence of the Lord is a wonderful thing. It is addictive. His presence is life and joy. When I am burdened by worries and fears, His presence washes them away in a moment. I feel cleansed by His presence, like a waterfall has washed away all my burdens.

People spend their lives trying to please God, but the sacrifices of religion are not acceptable to God. Mother Teresa tried to make her entire life a sacrifice to God. But what if the sacrifice she gave to God was a sacrifice not given in obedience to the Holy Spirit but in obedience to a religious spirit? Then the sacrifice is not acceptable to God. It is the sacrifice of Cain. It is a sacrifice that is rejected by God.

THE CROSSES OF RELIGION

Perhaps the greatest deception that religion has committed is causing people to give the wrong sacrifice - to carry the wrong cross. An Islamic terrorist thinks he is paying a high price for his God. He thinks he is taking up his cross and following the plan of God for his life. In fact, he is a slave of the Evil One, paying the highest price for the kingdom of darkness. This is the great deception of religion. Men pay a high price, but the price is the wrong price. It is not the price that God has asked them to pay.

Jesus said of the Pharisees **"…they bind heavy burdens, hard to bear, and lay them on men's shoulders; but they themselves will not move them with one of their fingers"** (Matthew 23:4).

Jesus called out to those who lived under these burdens, **"Come to Me, all you who labor and are heavy laden, and I will give you rest. Take My yoke upon you and learn from Me, for I am gentle and lowly in heart, and you will find rest for your souls. For My yoke is easy and My burden is light"** (Matthew 11:28-30).

The religious spirit puts a heavy burden, hard to bear, upon men's shoulders. This heavy burden is the false cross of religion, the price men pay as they obey the demands of religion. It is the offering of human striving, the offering of Cain that must be rejected by God.

Those who carry this burden are not helped by their religion. They pay a price, but there is nobody helping them to pay it. The burden becomes too much. It weighs them down. It depresses them and embitters them. The religious man becomes bitter inside as he pays a price for God, and yet God doesn't seem to accept his offering.

In contrast, the true child of God carries a cross because of thankfulness and love. This cross is the yoke that Jesus gives his disciples. It is an easy burden, a light burden, because it is the yoke of Jesus and he helps them to carry the burden.

What does this mean? When religion asks you to fast for 40 days, religion will not help you in your fast. The fast will be burdensome and dreary. You will spend your time thinking about the great price you are paying. You will find yourself becoming very annoyed at the people around you. There is no grace or power in this fast. When you finish this fast, you will be more bound by the spirit of religion than you were before you began.

The Bible teaches us that "you are the slaves of the one you obey" (Romans 6:16). If you obey a spirit of religion, and go on a long fast, you will become the slave of religion. The Muslim who obeys his religion and pays a price and fasts during the month of Ramadan will come under a greater bondage to his religion during that month. This is why Ramadan is often the time when Muslims commit acts of violence because of their religion.

In contrast, if you obey the Spirit of God, the Lord Himself is there to help you pay the price that He asks you to pay. If the Spirit of God asks you to go on a 40-day fast, that fast will not be so difficult. You will wake up in the morning feeling the joy of the Lord and the presence of the Lord. His presence will be so close to you that the price of the fast seems like a very light thing to carry. It is an easy yoke, a burden that is light.

This is the promise and joy of Christianity. Whatever God asks you to go through, He will go through it with you. Only Jesus Himself was forsaken at the cross because of the sin that he carried. Those who believe in Jesus and follow Him will never be forsaken. Even when we pass through the valley of the shadow of death, we will fear no evil because He is with us!

Life is too short to spend it serving religion!

APPENDIX

Personal Views on Military Service

Some readers may be trying to discern my own views regarding peace and nonresistance. I'll try to summarize them briefly here.

I believe that the kingdom of heaven will one day fill the earth and that the authority of Christ will rule over the nations. At the present time, I believe the kingdom of heaven rules in the hearts of people who choose Christ as Lord and Savior. The supernatural love and power of Christ changes men from the inside, turning their hearts from darkness to light.

The weapons of the kingdom are not the weapons of this world. The kingdom of heaven can never be advanced with swords or guns. This is why Jesus said, **"My kingdom is not of this world. If My kingdom were of this world, My servants would fight, so that I should not be delivered to the Jews; but now My kingdom is not from here"** (John 18:36).

Most of the teaching of Jesus was about the kingdom of heaven. He taught us about the supernatural love of His kingdom, a love that extends even to one's enemies. He taught us that His kingdom is never spread through man's violence. He taught us to turn the other cheek.

At the same time, until the day that Christ rules over the nations, earthly governments are very necessary. They cannot spread the kingdom of heaven. They cannot transform men's hearts with the supernatural love of god. They not given the weapons that are "mighty in God" as Paul described. They are given the sword.

The sword can only do certain things. It can never bring in the kingdom of heaven. It can never change men's hearts. The sword can only limit the spread of evil upon the earth to some degree. It can never remove the root of evil that lies in persons' hearts. It can only make evil people afraid to act upon their evil impulses.

The sword is not the tool of the kingdom of heaven. It always represents "the lesser of two evils." There is always a downside to using the sword. Nevertheless, if the sword is used wisely, it will save lives.

The governments of this world are given the sword, and the choices they face are almost always choices between the lesser of two evils. This is simply the nature of earthly governments, the nature of this age, until the day that Christ returns to rule the earth.

In other words, our government faced no good choices in Iraq, only bad and worse choices. Allowing Saddam Hussein to continue doing what he was doing was not a good choice. Invading Iraq was not a good choice. Politicians examined the choices and their flawed intelligence reports. Democrats and Republicans voted for the invasion in overwhelming majorities. In retrospect, the choice may have been wrong. The aggression of Saddam Hussein could likely have been contained without an invasion.

Likewise, Barack Obama viewed the choices in Iraq. Al Qaeda was largely defeated in Iraq. When Barack Obama took office, America was tired of war. Obama decided to withdraw nearly all American troops. In retrospect, this choice was wrong. As America pulled out completely, the defeated forces of extremist Islam came back to life in the form of Isis, which have spread an even more extreme form of genocide through the nations of the Middle East.

We are told to pray for our governments, not to condemn every move they make. It is easy to judge their decisions in retrospect without understanding the difficulty of the choices faced.

Lives are not always saved by withdrawals. Peace activists are always counting up the casualties caused by America's invasions. They never count the casualties caused by America's withdrawals, defeats, and betrayals of its allies.

In some situations, the aggressive, decisive use of military force will save the most lives on both sides of the conflict. If the French had taken decisive military action in 1936 when Hitler first tried to reoccupy the Rhineland, it might have cost them hundreds of lives, but millions of lives would likely have been saved. It is estimated that even the activation of a single French military division at that time could have stopped the Nazis. Likewise, the decisive, aggressive use of military force could have shortened the US Civil War by years and saved tens of thousands of lives on both sides of the divide. The destruction of a few boatloads of Somali pirates in 2005 could have stopped the formation of the Somali piracy industry, which has helped spread terrorism throughout East Africa. If these actions had been taken with decisive force at the right time, even the lives of many of America's enemies would have been saved by the swift conclusion of these conflicts.

Sometimes the least merciful option is to do nothing, standing back and merely watching as conflicts grow from a small fire into a grand conflagration. Sometimes the most costly option in warfare (in terms of lives) is to gradually enter a conflict with measured responses to aggression. This often results in a stalemate, a war that drags on year after year, costing far more lives than a brief, intensive decisive conflict would have.

The use of military force can be compared to modern medicine. When a doctor treats the sick, he is not really spreading the kingdom of heaven. He is not using the divine power, the supernatural miracles of that kingdom. He is not bringing people to God. He is using modern drugs and surgery to save lives.

The methods a doctor uses often represent "the lesser of two evils." The side effects of some drugs can be very severe, almost as severe as the diseases they are treating. Sometimes surgery kills the patient more quickly than the disease would have. And yet we are all thankful for doctors and modern medicine because we recognize that in spite of its limitations, it offers us a far better option than the alternative.

Likewise, soldiers are necessary. We should pray for political and military leaders that they might use the sword with wisdom, in a way that ultimately saves lives. We should not assume that the wise use of force means that our government does what the peace activists want them to do. We should understand that government force can never bring the kingdom of heaven to earth. Even if the government uses military force with great wisdom, there will be many negative side effects from what they do. Many innocent people were killed by US forces in World War II as they rained bombs down upon Western Europe. And yet the Allied military invasion of Europe represented the wise use of force. It was a much better option than the option of doing nothing and allowing the Nazi plague to continue spreading around the world.

It is a big mistake when the government of a nation tries to use the tools of the kingdom of heaven. The US government is not supposed to "turn the other cheek" or love its enemies. The government of the United States is given the sword by God and its job is to use that sword with wisdom. The government cannot change hearts. The government can only punish the extremes of evil. For example, the government cannot remove racism from the heart of a racist. The government can only deal with the man's violent actions. Only the love and power given to the church can change that man's heart. The government can kill many terrorists, but it cannot defeat the spiritual forces of Islam that inspire the terrorists.

Just as the US government should not try to use the love of God to achieve its purposes, the church should not use the sword to achieve its purposes. When the church tries to use the sword, the result is a "holy" crusade that is very unholy in reality. The medieval crusaders fought in the name of Christ as they slaughtered thousands of Jews and Muslim civilians. They fought with the belief that their crusade was holy and that their sins would be forgiven if they joined the crusade. This brought tremendous confusion in Europe and the Middle East regarding the true nature of Christianity and the kingdom of heaven.

In effect, the crusaders acted like Muslims, who believe that holy war (jihad) is an important part of their faith. The Christians of the Middle Ages responded to 500 years of Islamic aggression and jihad by fighting a jihad of their own. It would have been much better if they had left God and the cross out of their war and simply fought under the authority of the European states. When you add God's name to something that is unholy, you do not cause the unholy thing to become holy. You simply add blasphemy to your other sins.

To sum up, the kingdoms of this world are given the sword, and they need to use it wisely. If they use it wisely, it will save lives. This sword can accomplish some tasks. The sword can be used to kill Islamic terrorists, but it cannot defeat the spiritual forces of Islam. America has killed thousands of terrorists, but Islam has not been shaken by America's military victories. The spiritual forces of Islam can only be defeated by the divinely powerful weapons, wielded by the true messengers of God. Islam will fall when the saints overcome by the blood of the Lamb, by the word of their testimony, and by not loving their lives unto death.

SHOULD CHRISTIANS BE INVOLVED IN MILITARY SERVICE?

The above discussion leaves the question, should Christians be involved in the military? It may be very necessary for governments to use military force to stop terrorists and other aggressors, but does this mean that Christians should join those military forces?

There are two ways of looking at this question. Some say that Christians should honor the government's God-given authority, and join the military when the government asks them to. When a Christian does this, he is not fighting under the rules of the kingdom of heaven, which would require him to turn the other cheek. He is fighting under the rules and authority given to earthly governments, which require him to use the sword. While he is on duty, he fights against his enemies with the training and weapons he has been given, and when he is off duty he can pray for them.

Other Christians say that even if it is necessary for a government to use military force, Christians should not participate in the military. They believe that the commands of Christ regarding loving one's enemies and turning the other cheek simply prohibit such service.

Quite simply, these are not easy questions. I do not think it is wise for the church to make a law in favor of either of these viewpoints. I am simply not ready to say that all Christians should leave the US military. If they did so, I think the US military would become a far more destructive and lawless institution than it is today. I think the presence of Christians in the military helps the military to follow a higher standard of respect for human rights and obedience to the rule of law.

Likewise, I do not think it would be wise for the church to conclude that Christians should always obey their government and join the military when asked. What about the Christians in Nazi Germany? Should they have obeyed their government and joined the ranks of the Nazis? I don't think so. There is a time to say no to the demands of government.

Some questions are better left to individual conscience and the leading of the Holy Spirit. I am very grateful that we live in a nation that respects the religious beliefs of its citizens, a nation that has made space for conscientious objectors to follow their conscience. May it continue to be that way.

Personally, even when I was young, I felt the Lord offering me a choice. I was eighteen and was experimenting with karate. I felt the Holy Spirit telling me that I could continue studying self-defense but that there would always be someone who knew more than me.   Or, I could trust the Lord, and He would protect me. I chose to stop studying self-defense at that moment. I am glad that I did. Today I face situations that I don't think self-defense training would be of much help. I lead a missionary training school in East Africa, and we work in many different Islamic communities. Al Shabab, the Somali wing of Al Qaeda is active here. They attacked a nearby church with assault weapons and threw grenades in some open-air meetings. The police informed us that we were on the Al Shabab hit list, and we had some other evidence that this was true.

I have always felt the Lord's protection. In spite of the fact that we have between 40-50 people working on a daily basis in many different Islamic communities, we have always experienced divine protection. In spite of all the threats, nobody has been injured.

I know that I am not called to join the military. I know that I am called to preach the gospel of the kingdom of heaven, and I know that earthly weapons are not useful in my calling. At the same time, I do not want to judge the committed Christians who feel that God has led them into the military.

Of course, some will say, why not apply this same approach to the question of gay marriage? Why not let people follow their consciences and the leading of the Holy Spirit in this area as well? It is never the Holy Spirit that leads people into committing sexual immorality. Homosexual activity is always condemned, in both the Old and New Testaments. It is not an area that is left to individual leading or interpretation.

The Bible does not say that all soldiers will be cast into the lake of fire. The New Testament teaches us that the sexually immoral and homosexual offenders will be cast there (I Corinthians 6:9). In the following verse, I Corinthians 6:11, Paul says "And such were some of you. But you were washed, but you were sanctified, but you were justified in the name of the Lord Jesus and by the Spirit of our God." In other words, some believers were formerly homosexual offenders. They left that sin and that lifestyle, and their sins were washed away.

There is no New Testament record of Jesus asking Roman soldiers or other Roman officials to leave their profession after they became believers. Jesus honored a centurion in the Roman army as a great man of faith, greater than anyone He found in all of Israel. This man was not instructed to leave the military. Likewise, in Acts 10, another centurion in the Roman army by the name of Cornelius had a supernatural experience and came to faith in Christ. There is no record that he left the Roman army. The jailer described in Acts 13 continued working as a jailer after he came to faith.

Paul makes it clear that some Christians were formerly homosexuals. who repented. He does not say that some who were in the military repented and left the military. The biblical record simply does not place these things in the same category. The activity of one is always condemned in the very strongest terms every time that the subject comes up while the other is not.

ABOUT THE AUTHOR

Vaughn Martin is a missionary based in Brussels, Belgium, where he lives with his wife and three daughters. Vaughn spends much of his time working to start missionary training schools in various nations. The evangelistic efforts of these schools are focused on reaching Muslims and other unreached groups with the gospel of Jesus Christ. Vaughn has written a number of books, including *There is a Way Back*, *Transforming the Heart of Africa* and *The Day of the Lord.*

If you would like to invite Vaughn to minister to your church about Islamic Ministry, or the message of this book, you can reach him at the following email address: vaughnmartin7@gmail.com

4/2018

224